Four Essays on Romance

EDITED BY HERSCHEL BAKER

Four Essays on Romance

HARVARD UNIVERSITY PRESS
CAMBRIDGE, MASSACHUSETTS
1971

Distributed in Great Britain by Oxford University Press, London

Publication of this book has been
aided by a grant from the
Hyder Edward Rollins Fund

Library of Congress Catalog Card Number 77-152269

SBN 674-31475-1

Printed in the United States of America

Introduction

WHEN, IN *Paradise Regained* (II.359–361), the aging Milton casts a nostalgic backward glance at the

> Fairy Damsels met in Forest wide
> By Knights of Logres, or of Lyones,
> Lancelot or Pelleas, or Pellenore,

he poignantly evokes that great literature of fairy tale and magic whose persistent vitality supplies the subject of the essays in this little book. Needless to say, the importance of the subject is out of all proportion to the dimensions of the book; for although Romance, the dominant genre of secular literature throughout the later Middle Ages, has prompted floods of scholarship and speculation, it still bristles with unanswered problems of origin, development, and even definition. It has been regarded, for example, as the sentimentalization of the broad heroic tradition that embraces not only the *chansons de geste* but also Vergil and the Greek romances, as the recension of ancient Celtic themes, as the extraordinary creation of Chrétien de Troyes, as a vehicle for the ethical code of feudalism, as a celebration of the ideal of chivalric *avanture,* as a literature of wish-fulfillment built upon the archetypal motif of the quest that leads through danger to success.

An even wider diversity is discernible in those works that may be said to exemplify or draw upon or provide ingredients for the tradition of Romance. The same inclusive rubric accommodates the derring-do of *King Horn* and the spiritual exaltation of *Parzival,* Greene's hack work in *Pandosto* and Sidney's elegant trifling in *Arcadia,* the allegedly sober verities of Geoffrey of Monmouth's *Historia regum Britanniae* and Spenser's dark conceits, the poetry of *Sir Gawain and the Green Knight* and the sturdy prose of Malory, the limpid couplets of Chrétien's *Cligés* and the prosodic convolutions of *The Winter's Tale,* the relentless simplicity of *Guy of Warwick* and the immense artifice of *Orlando Furioso.*

When, for these and other reasons, I thought that Romance would be a useful, humbling topic for English Section I at the 1969 meeting of the Modern Language Association I was fortunate in persuading Professors Newstead, Giamatti, Rabkin, and Lewalski to abet the undertaking. Their papers, which are here printed substantially as they were read in Denver that December, not only serve to remind us of the deep resources of Romance: they also help us understand how great and widely separated writers have responded to a literary tradition that in its charm and richness and resilience must be regarded as one of the triumphs and the mysteries of European culture.

H.B.

Contents

HELAINE NEWSTEAD

Malory and Romance

THE SUBJECT OF THIS GROUP of essays is a literary genre that resists easy definition. Although the romance dominated medieval secular literature for some three hundred years, it was by no means a homogeneous body of material. Yet, we have grown accustomed to the term as a convenient label for narratives that differ widely in subject matter, treatment, style, and literary quality.[1] Because my subject concerns Malory and his relation to the genre, I shall concentrate on the Arthurian legends not only because they form the substance of his work but also because they are typical.

The modern connotations of the word romance—adventure and love—are distinctive elements in the French courtly romances. According to Auerbach's brilliant analysis,[2] the romance depicts an ideal courtly world, completely detached from political, economic, and historical realities, in which the knight seeks adventure in order to prove his worth. The surface of life in this ideal, heightened world, however, is described in realistic pictures of the ceremonies and customary rituals of hospitality and entertainment. Courtesy is expressed in observance of the rules of combat as well as in civility in social relations. Women are also important, and love is either the cause or the result of particular adventures. The life of trial by adventure is restricted to an élite, exclusive group pursuing an absolute ideal of personal, inner worth. Auerbach puts it this way: "Except feats of arms and love, nothing can occur in the courtly world—and even these two are of a special sort: they are not occurrences or emotions which can be absent for a time; they are permanently connected with the person of the perfect knight, they are part of his definition, so that he cannot for one moment be without adventure in arms nor for one moment be without amorous entanglement. If he could, he would lose himself and no longer be a knight." [3]

There are, of course, other approaches to the romance,[4] but Auerbach's interpretation is a useful starting point. The French concept of chivalry in the early romances was modified in the process of adaptation to English tastes and audiences, as we should expect, but even in France the chivalric ideal was challenged in the *Queste* and *Mort Artu* sections of the French Vulgate cycle[5] by the emphasis upon a supposedly superior religious chivalry. The focus of the courtly chivalric romances was further blurred in England by the quite different but equally potent tradition of Arthur as a historical king of Britain. Malory was familiar with this tradition, and his treatment of the romances was strongly colored by it. To explain its effect upon his work, I shall review some of its literary manifestations among his predecessors.

After the appearance of Geoffrey of Monmouth's sensational *History of the Kings of Britain* about 1136,[6] the glorious reign of King Arthur, his military conquests that extended his empire to Rome, and his tragic downfall through treachery of his nephew Mordred became fixed as part of British history. Geoffrey's Latin work spread the fame of Arthur among the learned, and the French version of the Norman poet Wace[7] made the legend familiar in courtly circles. Instead of knight-errantry, there are major wars against the heathen Saxons and other national foes, and Arthur himself is the military leader, a monarch surrounded by vassal kings. Love is of no significance in the events recounted except for a passing reference or so. There is a fundamental distinction, as Auerbach points out, between warfare for political and economic reasons, as in Geoffrey's *Historia,* and the feats of arms performed by the individual knight in the romances. Geoffrey's *Historia* may be as fictitious as the romances of Chrétien, but his model was Latin historiography, and his sober, plausible style carries the conviction of truth. Wace has a similar aim, though he writes in the metrical form of the romance and embellishes the narrative with descriptions directed to the taste of a courtly audience. Neither work, however, is properly a romance.

The first English Arthurian poem, Layamon's *Brut,*[8] represents an even more startling deviation from the spirit of courtly French romance. Layamon transforms Wace's narrative into an English heroic poem, composed in the language, style, and alliterative meter of native English verse. The subject matter is the same, but the style, inherited from Anglo-Saxon poetic tradition, and the passionate celebration of warfare set it apart from its predecessors. Arthur is Britain's darling, a warrior-king, who exults in battle, exhorts his valiant thanes, and taunts his enemies, rejoicing that their souls are consigned to hell. The battle scenes are elaborated with a joyous gusto in details of carnage that some critics consider barbarous.[9] Nevertheless, Arthur has other qualities of a heroic king: he is generous to his vassals, magnanimous to conquered foes who submit to him, and compassionate toward the suffering of innocent victims. Although Layamon's poem records some marvels, such as the belief in Arthur's eventual return,[10] the tone is that of a heroic poem rather than a romance.

In Layamon, as well as in Geoffrey and Wace, the story of Arthur is only a part of the history of British kings from Brutus to the last of Arthur's successors. The heroic concept of Arthur represented by Layamon's treatment must have continued in English poetry for it emerges in the late fourteenth century in the alliterative *Morte Arthure*,[11] a poem independent of Layamon, but composed in the same metrical tradition. The Arthuriad is here detached from the rest of British history, and the story is reshaped in the form of a medieval tragedy, recounting the triumphs of Arthur as a mighty conqueror and his lamentable fall and death. The story is derived from Wace, with liberal additions from the legends of Alexander, Charlemagne, and other non-Arthurian sources.[12] The effect is to magnify Arthur as the invincible leader of imperial conquests and to define by contrast the tragic significance of his downfall.

The war with Rome is the principal subject of the poem. When the Roman emperor demands tribute, Arthur is already the conqueror of many lands from Ireland to Austria. In the battles that follow his rejection of the emperor's arrogant claim, Arthur is depicted as a Christian king fighting a war against a foe allied with Moslems, heathen, and giants. The knights of the Round Table under his leadership perform prodigies of valor, but it is Arthur himself who slays the emperor. At the moment of triumph, as he prepares to be crowned in Rome, he has an ominous dream of Fortune's wheel, which prophesies his imminent downfall and death. The news of Mordred's treachery follows immediately, and the prophecy of doom is swiftly fulfilled after Arthur's return to Britain in the disasters that lead to his death. He is buried with appropriate ceremony in Glastonbury by his grieving survivors.

Arthur dominates the poem. Though he can be ruthlessly cruel to his foes, he is generous and hospitable to vassals, friends, and emissaries. In the dream of Fortune's wheel (vv. 3218–3455), which is central to the meaning of the poem, Arthur moves beyond the limits of British history into the illustrious company of the Nine Worthies, world conquerors who are likewise doomed to fall from the heights of earthly glory.

This is no poem for the squeamish. Its values of prowess and loyalty are uncompromisingly military, and revenge is a common motive that no one questions. After the dying Arthur solemnly offers thanks to God for all his victories, he orders the merciless drowning of Mordred's children and then declares his forgiveness of all wrongs for God's love (vv. 4295–4325). It is a hero's death as glorious as his life, with no hint of repentance for sin.

Loyalty is as much prized as valor. It is manifest in the actions of the Round Table knights in battle, and Mordred's treason is the more heinous because of the supreme value of loyalty. The relation of the king to his knights is movingly expressed in his lament for his fallen warriors:

> Here rystys the riche blude   of the rownde table,
> Rebukkede with a rebawde,   and rewthe es the more!
> I may helples one hethe   house be myn one
> Als a wafull wedowe,   þat wanttes hir beryn.
> I may werye and wepe   and wrynge myn handys,
> For my wytt and my wyrchipe   awaye es for euer.
> Off all lordchips I take   leue to myn ende;

Here es þe Bretons blode   broughte owt of lyfe,
And nowe in þis journee   all my joy endys!

(vv. 4282–4290)

Arthur's glory comes to an end when his fellowship of knights is destroyed.

The alliterative *Morte Arthure* is both a heroic poem and a tragedy. It is not concerned with the romance themes of love and individual adventure to prove a knight's inner worth. Instead, its themes are large-scale warfare for political ends and actions with a public rather than a personal significance. The interpretation of the Arthurian story as tragedy was not confined, however, to the alliterative *Morte Arthure*. In the French prose *Mort Artu*,[13] the final section of the prose *Lancelot,* the theme of inexorable destiny shapes the close of Arthur's reign. Before the final battle with Mordred, Arthur has a dream of Fortune and her wheel, which presages his doom. But the Nine Worthies do not appear, and the dream occurs at a moment when Arthur's fortunes are already on the wane. Although the effect is somewhat different, the dream of Fortune's wheel in both suggests that it was natural to see in Arthur's rise and fall, as related by Geoffrey and Wace, the pattern of medieval tragedy.

Malory knew and used both the alliterative *Morte Arthure* and the French *Mort Artu*. He uses the English poem in his account of the Roman wars, the second Tale in Vinaver's edition of Malory,[14] but he turns to the *Mort Artu* version for the conclusion of the whole work because the principal hero of the French romance is Lancelot, his paragon of chivalry. In Malory's version, as in the *Mort Artu,* the death of Arthur is followed by the death of Lancelot. But literary

8

influences cannot be measured quantitatively. Although most of Malory's sources were his voluminous French books, the influence of the alliterative *Morte Arthure* was more pervasive than one would suppose from its adaptation in the *Tale of Arthur and Lucius.*

This Tale, though it stands second in the sequence, was the first to be composed.[15] In the alliterative *Morte Arthure* Malory found much that was congenial to his temperament. It was, first of all, a straightforward narrative, free from the interlacing techniques typical of the French prose romances. It evoked the glories of Arthur's career in vigorous action and colloquial, dramatic speech. It depicted with powerful immediacy the emotional force of the loyalties binding together the king and his military fellowship in such scenes as Arthur's passionate threnody for the dead Gawain (vv. 3949–4024) and young Idrus' refusal to leave the king's side in battle even to help his endangered father.[16] In the heroic world of the English poem men are responsible for their actions, and actions are judged by their public significance. There is no room for courtly love or for magic and the supernatural. Such attitudes are not without influence upon Malory's treatment of his material.

Malory's French sources are romances, different in outlook and structure. They contain a profusion of adventures of knight-errantry and love narrated according to the interwoven techniques that distinguish the French prose cycles. Malory tries to follow the natural order of events in a story, assembling incidents often widely separated in the French. He does not always succeed, but his preference is unmistakable.[17] In addition, he omits and condenses whatever seems to impede the action, so that the effect, whether intended or not, is similar to the swiftly moving scenes of the *Morte Arthure*. He seeks clarification in other ways, too, by naming anonymous knights,[18] by announcing the identity of a knight at once instead of deferring the revelation in the French manner,[19] and by assigning names, most of them English, to localities left vague in the original.[20]

He also reduces the importance of the supernatural element, when he cannot remove it entirely. Magical incidents are narrated as though they were quite ordinary events, as in this account of Merlin's entombment:

Than sone aftir the lady and Merlyon departed. And by weyes he shewed hir many wondyrs, and so come into Cornuayle. And allwayes he lay aboute to have hir maydynhode, and she was ever passynge wery of hym and wolde have bene delyverde of hym, for she was aferde of hym for cause he was a devyls son, and she cowde not be skyfte of hym by no meane. And so one a tyme Merlyon ded shew hir in a roche whereas was a grete wondir and wrought by enchauntement that went undir a grete stone. So by hir subtyle worchying she made Merlyon to go undir that stone to latte hir wete of the mervayles there, but she wrought so there for hym that he come never oute for all the craufte he coude do, and so she departed and leffte Merlyon.[21]

This kind of treatment strips the romantic glamour from such figures as Merlin and Morgan, so that in Malory they are significant chiefly as friend and foe of Arthur. The matter-of-fact manner contributes strongly to the impression of plausibility and veracity that marks Malory's style.

In the multitude of knightly adventures drawn from the

French prose romances, the early ideas of courtly chivalry are modified to conform to Malory's more heroic concept. The individual knight seeks adventure to prove his worth, but in Malory this quality is no private virtue but rather honor or worship,[22] the high reputation among his peers earned for deeds of valor. The most worshipful become members of the Round Table fellowship; they owe loyalty to one another and, above all, to King Arthur. When Arthur establishes the Round Table, he charges the knights

never to do outerage nothir morthir, and allwayes to fle treson, and to gyff mercy unto hym that askith mercy, uppon payne of forfiture [of their] worship and lordship of kynge Arthure for evirmore; and allwayes to do ladyes, damesels, and jantilwomen and wydowes [socour:] strengthe hem in hir ryghtes, and never to enforce them, uppon payne of dethe. Also, that no man take no batayles in a wrongefull quarell for no love ne for no worldis goodis.[23]

This oath is solemnly renewed each year at the feast of Pentecost. Since this famous passage is Malory's addition, it seems to represent his own view of chivalry. If the knights do not always adhere to this ideal code, at least they are all aware of it. It rests, of course, upon deeds of physical prowess, and a knight's reputation is a matter of public recognition. Lancelot's preeminence is generally acknowledged, and it is no accident that he first distinguishes himself as a valiant warrior in the war against the Romans,[24] not as Guinevere's lover, as in the French. In Malory's work love occupies a secondary place. His code of chivalry warns against wrongful battles undertaken for love and classifies them in the same category as those for sordid gain. Love plays a part in many stories, to be sure, but he omits or drastically condenses introspective and lyrical passages dealing with love, its anguish and its rapture.[25] Lancelot's love for Guinevere is imagined in Malory as a kind of loyalty akin to that which Lancelot cherishes for the king.

It is not so much the fact of adultery as its public disclosure that brings shame and dishonor to both Arthur and Guinevere and that inspires Lancelot's gallant lies to shield her reputation and his brilliant defense against the armed knights who surprise him in the queen's bedchamber. Arthur's comment on this exploit is hardly that of an outraged husband:

"Jesu mercy!" seyde the kynge, "he ys a mervaylous knyght of proues. And alas," seyde the kynge, "me sore repentith that ever sir Launcelot sholde be ayenste me, for now I am sure the noble felyshyp of the Rounde Table ys brokyn for ever, for wyth hym woll many a noble knyght holde. And now hit ys fallen so," seyde the kynge, "that I may nat with my worshyp but my quene muste suffir dethe," and was sore amoved.[26]

The priorities are clear: Lancelot's prowess and the Round Table fellowship are far more precious than the queen, whose dismal fate is mentioned almost as an afterthought. Arthur expresses the same view later after Lancelot's rescue of the queen and his inadvertent slaying of Gareth: "And much more I am soryar for my good knyghtes losse than for the losse of my fayre quene; for quenys I myght have inow, but such a felyship of good knyghtes shall never be togydirs in no company." [27]

The fellowship disintegrates because of Mordred's treason and Gawain's implacable insistence on vengeance for the death of his brother Gareth. In the bitter strife, Lancelot maintains his heroic loyalty to the king, despite extreme provocation and deadly insult. At the end, it is Lancelot who is left to mourn, offering prayers at the tomb of Gawain, and burying Guinevere by the side of King Arthur in Glastonbury. He spends his last days mourning by their tomb in grief that cannot be assuaged. When the hermit reminds him that such sorrow might be displeasing to God, he replies:

I trust I do not dysplese God, for He knoweth myn entente: for my sorow was not, nor is not, for ony rejoysyng of synne, but my sorow may never have ende. For whan I remembre of hir beaulté and of hir noblesse, that was bothe wyth hyr kyng and wyth hyr, so whan I sawe his corps and hir corps so lye togyders, truly myn herte wold not serve to susteyne my careful body. Also whan I remembre me how by my defaute and myn orgule and my pryde that they were bothe layed ful lowe, that were pereles that ever was lyvyng of Cristen people, wyt you wel . . . this remembred, of their kyndenes and myn unkyndenes, sanke so to myn herte that I myght not susteyne myself.[28]

The whole concluding section is an extended elegy for the vanished glories of the Arthurian fellowship. Lancelot's bleak desolation recalls the striking passage at the end of the alliterative *Morte Arthure* in which Arthur likens his plight to that of a woeful widow alone on a heath longing vainly for her lord. Although Lancelot dies as a hermit, Sir Hector's eloquent threnody for him evokes his matchless chivalry, ending with these words: "And thou were the sternest knyght to thy mortal foo that ever put spere in the reeste." [29] The final image of Lancelot in battle leaves us with the powerful impression of his heroic energy, the same quality that marked his first appearance as a young knight in the Roman wars.

There are echoes of the alliterative *Morte Arthure* in the threnody for Lancelot as there are elsewhere in the conclusion.[30] They direct attention to the heroic temper of Malory's conception of the Arthurian story. The diversity of incident in the whole long work fails to obscure the outline of medieval tragedy in the rise and fall of the Arthurian world. Its values are embodied in the Round Table fellowship in the secular virtues of prowess, loyalty, and honor expressed in terms of action and public significance. To be aware of the heroic strain in Malory is to understand much in his work that runs counter to the spirit of romance, for to Malory the story of Arthur had the dignity of history. Looking back upon the heroic past, he conveys the truth of the experience as he understood it by expressing the sense of profound loss that is the only response to the passing of splendor.

A. BARTLETT GIAMATTI

Spenser: From Magic to Miracle

"WE ARE ON ENCHANTED GROUND, MY FRIEND," says Bishop Hurd of Romance in the sixth of his *Letters on Chivalry and Romance:* a world, he says later of the Italian poets, where "anything is enough to be the basis for their air-form'd visions" (Letter X). But, if Hurd recognizes the visionary part of Romance, he also knows that reason is gaining ascendancy "over the portentous spectres of the imagination . . . So that Milton, as fond as we have seen he was of the Gothic fictions, durst only admit them of the bye, and in the way of simile and illustration only." "Instead of Giants and Magicians," says Hurd of Milton, "he had Angels and Devils to supply him with the *marvelous,* with greater probability" (Letter XII).[1]

I want to survey that "enchanted ground" from a particular vantage point. My perspective on the chivalric romances of Spenser and his Italian predecessors will be on perspective in those poems, on one of the ways the poems deal with the problem of seeing and the necessities for sight. Though not in the manner of Bishop Hurd, I will be concerned with Romance's visionary part, with how and what one sees when standing on enchanted ground. And my argument will be that throughout the tradition of chivalric romance one is offered moments of divine vision or revelation, visions connected with the simple gesture of raising a visor or a helmet. Thus, when a poet like Milton, in Hurd's language, substitutes the Christian marvelous for Gothic enchantment, we are not witnessing a radical break with the past so much as the completion of an impulse implicit in chivalric romance all along.

This impulse to reveal divinity is manifest when a visor or

17

helmet is raised.[2] At that moment the reader, or protagonist, of chivalric romance—or both—discovers an image of permanence and perfection through the reconciliation of opposites. These versions of stability, of certainty, are so crucial because they are what Romance, at its heart, constantly yearns for.

The world of Romance is always seen as in flux and of flux, a world where change, reversal, and discovery work through Time, Time whose power, we are reminded in *The Winter's Tale,* is

To o'erthrow law, and in one self-born hour
To plant and o'erwhelm custom.   (IV.i.8–9)

It is a world where the enchanted ground is always shifting. Within this flux lies Romance's visionary core, whose burning integrity, if only we can perceive it, can redeem the ravages of mortality. When in chivalric romance the moment of vision or revelation occurs, we are summoned from shimmering vistas of magic to stable peaks of miracle. We are delivered, if only briefly, from the sway of Ovid to the certainties of Vergil. Ovid is the patron saint of Romance mutability, Vergil the father of its visionary core. The narrative modes of Romance are all implicit in Daphne's flight from Apollo, while Romance's visionary impulse, its radical hunger for certainty and divinity, is incarnate in Venus, revealed as a goddess to her errant, baffled son. Ovid stands behind the Angelicas and Florimells fleeing their tormentors; Vergil behind Hermione stepping down to Perdita.

Before surveying the momentary transformations of magic

into miracle in *The Faerie Queene,* we will glance at some Italian poets. My apology for the necessarily allusive nature of this essay is that, with Astolfo, I have found the only way to cover enchanted ground is by hippogriff.

In canto 32 of Ariosto's *Orlando Furioso,*[3] Bradamante reveals herself. First there is jesting about the shining hair of Britomart's great precursor:

La donna cominciando a disarmarsi
L'avea lo scudo e dipoi l'elmo tratto;
Quando una cuffia d'oro, in che celarsi
Soleano i capei lunghi e star di piatto,
Uscí con l'elmo; onde caderon sparsi
Giù per le spalle, e la scopriro a un tratto
E la feron conoscer per donzella,
Non men che fiero in arme, in viso bella.

The woman began to disarm herself;
First her shield, then her helmet she took off;
When a golden hairnet, in which her long hair
Usually hid itself and stayed in place,
Fell with the helmet; whence the hair fell
Down to her shoulders and revealed her suddenly
And made her known as a maiden,
No less beautiful of face than fierce in arms.   (79)

As is often the case with this motif, the revelation is communicated in terms of opposites reconciled, here a masculine might and a feminine beauty contained and displayed in the single figure of Bradamante. Ariosto, however, further refines our perception of this revelation in the next octave.

Quale a cader de le cortine suole
Parer fra mille lampade la scena,
D'archi, e di più una superba mole,
D'oro, e di statue, e di pittura piena;
O come suol fuor de le nube il sole
Scoprir la faccia limpida e serena,
Così l'elmo levandosi dal viso
Mostrò la donna aprisse il paradiso.

As when a theater curtain customarily falls aside,
The scene appears amidst a thousand lamps,
Full of arches, and then a splendid hill,
And statues of gold and pictures;
Or when the sun is accustomed through clouds
To discover its face glistening and serene;
So the helmet, raised from the face,
Showed the woman, opened paradise.   (80)

The simile of the theater curtain, from Ovid (*Met.* III.111–114), communicates the sudden, brilliant completeness of the revelation, while the simile of the sun, shining clear and serene through clouds, shifts our gaze, again through glistening light, to the heavens. The last couplet completes the analogy and then, as the syntax collapses, identifies Bradamante with paradise. The maiden herself is now an image of that happy place.[4]

These paradoxes reconciling opposites, the images of light, the promise of paradise, are the common terms of Boiardo, Ariosto's master in the world of chivalric romance. Near the end of his massive *Orlando Innamorato* (III.v.38), Boiardo says that Bradamante wanted to see Ruggiero's visor-covered face more than she wanted to see paradise itself.[5] And when three octaves later she reveals her face to him through an upraised visor, we hear of her golden hair, but more of her face, where "a certain delicacy / Was mixed with vigor and strong desire" ("una delicatezza / Mescolata di ardire e di vigore") (41). Her "angelic face" (42) combines divinity and humanity, strength and tenderness, male and female, in a vision so perfect, Boiardo says, he cannot even describe it (41).

Ariosto and Boiardo present us with a Camilla who then reveals herself as a kind of Beatrice. Indeed it is to Dante's Beatrice we must turn, for from her revelation to the pilgrim in Eden the Italian poets, and thence others, derive their language of vision and their image of a woman who embodies bliss beyond the reach of change.

In *Purgatory* XXX,[6] preceded by the words which presaged Christ, Beatrice is revealed to her trembling lover:

> Io vidi già nel cominciar del giorno
>   la parte orïental tutta rosata,
>   e l'altro ciel di bel sereno adorno;
> e la faccia del sol nascere ombrata,
>   sì che, per temperanza di vapori,
>   l'occhio la sostenea lunga fiata:
> cosi dentro una nuvola di fiori
>   che dalle mani angeliche saliva
>   e ricadeva in giù dentro e di fori,
> sovra candido vel cinta d'uliva
>   donna m'apparve, sotto verde manto
>   vestita di color di fiamma viva.

> I once saw at the beginning of the day,
>   the eastern part of the sky all rosy
>   and the rest clear and beautiful;
> And the face of the sun came forth shaded
>   so that through the tempering vapours
>   the eye could bear it long;
> So within a cloud of flowers,
>   which rose from the angel's hands
>   and fell again within and without,
> A lady appeared to me, bound with olive
>   over a white veil, clothed under a green mantle
>   with the color of flame.   (22–33)

Only later will Dante see directly: now he looks through veils, as if seeing the sun through clouds. But the language and, I would argue, the significance of the profound revelation are adapted by the poets of chivalric romance for their visions discovered through a raised visor or discarded helmet. No Beatrice is Bradamante; but her magic armor can still reveal miracle.

In the third canto of his *Morgante,* the first of the great Italian writers of Romance, Luigi Pulci,[7] tells us how the ubiquitous Roland wounds a knight; it is the girl Meridïana.

> l'elmo gli uscì, la treccia si vedea,
> che raggia come stelle per sereno,
> anzi pareva di Venere iddea,
> anzi quella che è fatta un alloro,
> anzi parea d'argento, anzi pur d'oro.
>
> the helmet falls, he sees the hair
> which shines like stars in the heavens;
> in fact, she looks like the goddess Venus;

in fact, like the girl who was made a laurel;
in fact, like silver; in fact, like gold.   (17)

Pulci, whose facial expression is always something between a
sneer and a tired smile, discovers for us the classical roots of
this tradition of revelation. Not in the figure of Daphne, here
because in *Metamorphoses* I her golden hair is emphasized
on three occasions (477, 497, 542), but in Venus and in the
gold and silver. For behind Pulci, and all the poets we have
noted, are the revelations of Venus to Aeneas and of Aeneas
to Dido in Book I of the *Aeneid*.[8] First the goddess:

> Dixit et avertens rosea cervice refulsit,
> ambrosiaeque comae divinum vertice odorem
> spiravere; pedes vestis defluxit ad imos,
> et vera incessu patuit dea.

> She spoke, and as she turned her rosy neck flashed
> and from her head ambrosial hair breathed divine fragrance,
> her garment fell around her feet,
> and where she walked she was revealed, a true goddess.
> (402–405)

Later, her godlike son steps from his surrounding cloud:

> restitit Aeneas claraque in luce refulsit,
> os umerosque deo similis; namque ipsa decoram
> caesariem nato genetrix lumenque iuventae
> purpureum et laetos oculis adflarat honores;
> quale manus addunt ebori decus, aut ubi flavo
> argentum Pariusve lapis circumdatur auro.

> Aeneas stood forth, and gleamed bright in the clear light,
> in shape and face like a god; his mother had given

23

him the beauty of flowing hair, and youth's ripe bloom,
And in his eyes a joyous light—like the sheen the hand
gives ivory, or when silver or Parian marble is set in gold.
(588–593)

Both Vergilian passages, emphasizing revelations through
veils or clouds of shining faces and hair, underscore divinity,
and derive from the moment Venus first appears, disguised,
to Aeneas:

o—quam te memorem, virgo? namque haud tibi voltus
mortalis, nec vox hominem sonat; o dea certe!

But what shall I call you, o maiden?—neither your
face is mortal, nor has your voice a human ring;
O surely a goddess!   (I.327–328)

O dea certe: the chivalric romance will dis-cover goddesses
through cloudy veils, and visors, and each revelation will
offer an instance of miraculous stability in a world of cease-
less change.[9] My aim, however, is not to track the spoor of
sources, nor hermetically to seal "influences"; I want simply
to identify an impulse animating chivalric romance in the
Renaissance so as better to approach some motifs Spenser
uses, for his own particular purposes, in *The Faerie Queene.*

Moments of vision or revelation are much more frequent,
and dense, in *The Faerie Queene* than in any preceding
Romance; we are constantly offered such moments, from the
primary level of visors raised and veils laid aside, to the grand
visions in the tenth cantos of Books I, IV, and VI or the

dream at Isis Church in V.vii. These moments recur so frequently because in this world of corrosive mutability, they are at once so evanescent and yet so necessary and desired. The poet constantly returns to these moments because Spenser's whole impulse is to flesh out the ideal, to grapple, or moor, the visionary to the real world; he is forever seeking a language, a grammar, that will be sufficiently suggestive and rare, even incantatory, and yet supple and generously mundane enough to capture and hold these moments of revelation intact. Where the Italian poets tended to concentrate on the effect of the vision or revelation on the beholder,[10] Spenser, with crucial and obvious exceptions, usually fastens on the quality of the vision itself.

By holding these moments aloft, as it were, Spenser hopes to discover permanence behind change and thus shape the perspective of his reader. The poet's goal is to teach us to distinguish between magic and miracle, between what is only vain appearance and a moment of divinity. He wants to reform our sight from that of *voyeurs* to that of *voyants,* from the gaze of spies to the vision of seers, always teaching us to see at once beneath and beyond what appears.

I can do no more than sketch the way these moments of divinity work in *The Faerie Queene.* In Book I, canto iii, our single gesture reveals two very different perspectives. At stanza 38, Sansloy overcomes a knight:

> rudely rending vp his helmet, [he] would
> Haue slaine him straight; but when he sees his age,
> And hoarie head of *Archimago* old,
> His hastie hand he doth amazed hold.

Contrasted with this revelation of falsity incarnate is the vision of truth some thirty stanzas earlier, when Una, "farre from all mens sight,"

> From her faire head her fillet she vndight,
> And laid her stole aside. Her angels face
> As the great eye of heauen shyned bright,
> And made a sunshine in the shadie place;
> Did neuer mortall eye behold such heauenly grace.   (4)

By contrasting the revelations of Archimago to Sansloy and of Una to the reader, Spenser is educating us to the fact that not all revelations are the same; not all are benign.[11] In this poem, a single gesture or impulse or activity can lead in completely opposite directions: context is all, wherein we must exercise our wary judgment. For instance, compare the two dream visions of beloved women in Book I: Red Cross's in I.i.47–50, Arthur's in I.ix.13–15. Because Red Cross believes what he sees, he earns Duessa and eventually despair; whereas Arthur, after his dream of the Faery Queene, offers us an image of the whole poem's effort to incarnate an ideal:

> From that day forth I lou'd that face diuine;
> From that day forth I cast in carfull mind,
> To seek her out with labour and long tyne,
> And neuer vow to rest, till her I fynd.   (I.ix.15)

Arthur's effort to make the divine face human; the poet's effort to grapple vision to the world with words, is parodied in Book II when Braggadocchio attempts to ravish Belphoebe (II.iii.42) and is reaffirmed when Arthur notes the Faerie Queene's "full lively" image on Guyon's shield in canto ix, stanza 3.[12]

Books I and II introduce us, then, to the difficult process of distinguishing kinds of magic from shapes of miracle, and of making miracle permanent in mutable human affairs; Books III, IV, and V embody this process, and thus parallel the quest of Arthur, in the figures of Britomart and Artegall. As was Bradamante in the Italian romances, Britomart will be the conduit for much of the poem's visionary energy. In her, as Spenser says at III.i.46, "aimiable grace, / and manly terrour mixed therewithall," [13] and at Malbecco's, at canto ix, after "vailed was her loftie crest" (st. 20), the guests are fixed

In contemplation of diuinitie:
But most they maruailed at her cheualree
and noble prowesse. (24)

Reconciling the opposites of male strength and feminine grace, at once an object of contemplation and a model of active power, she embodies a Renaissance version of perfection. But it is Britomart's face, blazing through her visor, that reveals her divinity throughout, and the language of the description at III.i.42–43, not only recalls the images of the Italian poets but also anticipates the language of the visions through her visor used at III.ix.20, IV.i.13, and IV.vi.22.

[She] vented vp her vmbriere,
And so did let her goodly visage to appere.

As when faire *Cynthia,* in darksome night,
Is in a noyous cloud enueloped,
Where she may find the substaunce thin and light,
Breakes forth her siluer beames, and her bright hed
Discouers to the world discomfited;
Of the poore traueller, that went astray,
With thousand blessing she is heried;
Such was the beautie and the shining ray,
With which faire *Britomart* gaue light vnto the day.
(III.i.42–43)

The image of her face, shining as does the moon through clouds, participates in more than a tradition of romance imagery. These lines, promising steadfastness in terms of guidance to weary travelers, recall all those images in *The Faerie Queene* and the *Epithalamium* of fixed stars guiding wanderers and of lodestars hidden behind clouds—images of beneficent or lost fixity, unconnected to visors or veils, which seem to come from the poet's deepest being.[14]

While Britomart appears perfect and steadfast, she seeks, like Arthur, to realize a vision of love. For she saw in her father's "mirrhour fayre"

A comely knight, all arm'd in complete wize,
Through whose bright ventayle, lifted vp on hye,
His manly face, that did his foes agrize,
And friends to termes of gentle truce entize,
Lookt forth . . .   (III.ii.24)

It is Artegall's face, like Phoebus out of the East.

Thus in the first two cantos of Book III, we have two revelations through visors: one of Britomart and one to Britomart. She must now match her face to his, and in tempering

Artegall's power with her chaste, affectionate grace effect a perfect union. The process of accommodating ideal opposites to human form is a long one and never permanently accomplished in this world of change for this pair any more than any other. But there is a moment in Book IV when vision is made flesh, when what we want and what we can have fleetingly meet. In canto vi of Book IV, Artegall unknowingly smites Britomart:

> Her ventayle shard away. . . .
> With that her angels face, vnseen afore,
> Like to the ruddie morne appeard in sight,
> Deawed with siluer drops, through sweating sore.   (19)

The divine face is made human by the sweat, those silver drops which in themselves reconcile the orders of art and nature. And when he sees this face at once angelic and earthly, Artegall

> At last fell humbly downe vpon his knee,
> And of his wonder made religion.   (22)

Wonder made religion—here magic is made miracle; this is the heart of Romance as by Revelation we apprehend divinity and comprehend steadfastness out of flux and shadowy ignorance.

There will be other discoveries in the poem: most notably Artegall, at V.v.12–13, will see Radigund through a visor as he saw Britomart and will succumb to pity, where once he knelt before a kind of grace.[15] And visions will abound in Book VI, not those through a visor, but visions of a wider, more communal kind as befits Courtesy—visions of women ringed in harmony: Elizabeth by courtiers in the Proem (st. 7), Serena ringed by savages at canto viii.39; Pastorella by shepherds in canto ix.8, and the girl ringed by graces and maidens on Mount Acidale in canto x.12. Indeed, the shepherds around Pastorella who "oft for wonder shout":

> As if some miracle of heauenly hew
> Were downe to them descended in that earthly vew   (VI.ix.8)

have made their wonder, religion. They have seen miracle incarnate on the enchanted ground, and in their "shouts" of joy the maker of Colin Clout may have both concealed his deepest hopes and revealed his despair at finding a language to express what they saw.[16]

The visor that conceals and reveals divinity is simply a chivalric variant on the Silenus Alcibiades, that statuette mentioned by Plato (*Symposium,* 215) whose crude exterior hid the luminous god. This figure, like the image of the husk and the kernel, was a favorite Renaissance emblem for poetry, and whole poems.[17] In this sense, *The Faerie Queene* is a Silenus, for Spenser—exploiting the language of veils and vision—directs us to lovely truth hidden in his poem.

> Vfitly I these ydle rimes present,
> The labor of lost time, and wit vnstayd:
> Yet if their deeper sence be inly wayd,
> And the dim vele, with which from comune vew
> Their fairer parts are hid, aside be layd.
> Perhaps not vaine they may appeare to you.
> (Commendatory sonnet to Lord Burleigh)

To sum up the significance of the visor and of vision and revelation in the romances of Spenser and his Italian predecessors, we can do no better than cite the poet who knew them best and surpassed them. At the beginning of Book III of *Paradise Lost,* Milton says:

> Thus with the year
> Seasons return, but not to me returns
> Day, or the sweet approach of Ev'n or Morn,
> Or sight of vernal bloom, or Summer's Rose,
> Or flocks, or herds, or human face divine;
> But cloud instead, and ever-during dark
> Surrounds me . . .
> So much the rather thou Celestial Light
> Shine inward, and the mind through all her powers
> Irradiate, there plant eyes, all mist from thence
> Purge and disperse, that I may see and tell
> Of things invisible to mortal sight. (40–46, 51–55)

In the raising of a visor, and all it means, we may see things invisible to mortal sight in revelations of the human face divine shining through, purging and dispersing, the clouds. For Spenser the discovery of that divine face made human represents the evanescent moment to which he constantly returns, as he tries to seize the moment through language and thus reform the deformations wrought by Time and chance and change. Like Prince Arthur, his Roland, his Aeneas, Spenser strives to find a way to make the vision real; for, like his hero, Spenser wants to raise the final visor, lay aside the final dim veil, finally discover the face he worshiped most, the true and abiding face of his Queen, and of her green and pleasant land.

NORMAN RABKIN

The Holy Sinner and the Confidence Man: Illusion in Shakespeare's Romances

ONE MIGHT THINK THAT SHAKESPEARE's last plays were no longer an enigma. We agree that they are "romances"; therefore we need no longer be dismayed by their confusion of genres, their mingling of sophisticated poetry and naive structure, their susceptibility to criticism which sees them either as religious expressions of Shakespeare's final wisdom or as experiments in conventions associated with a naive popular mode a decade out of fashion and with a meretricious new kind of play just slinking out of the coterie theaters. Because we know that we understand more than Strachey did when he saw them as a fitful and abortive retreat into the valueless haven of fairy tale, because we recognize the mastery of Shakespeare's technique at countless moments and in countless ways, we have agreed not to view these plays as problematic, and confidence in Shakespeare's mastery has made possible a generation of brilliant criticism.

But such criticism has succeeded by a comfortable assumption that whatever part the critic happens to be exploring constitutes the whole, and it has consistently evaded what must remain for most the chief problem in knowing how to respond to the last plays. On one level each of these plays is concerned with the creation of a world that can be interpreted as we interpret the world of any of the earlier plays. In that world, as in any Shakespearean world, character and destiny are aspects of a cosmos whose laws operate the action of the play, and our illusion is that we are participating in a life that has its own full and peculiar integrity. Thus, when in *The Winter's Tale* we see the tragedy of middle age dissolve into the comedy of youth at a sheep-shearing, we remember that before the tragic events, through the dark backward and abysm of time, Leontes and Polixenes had spent a childhood like the childhood of Florizel and Perdita, "as twinned lambs that did frisk i' th' sun,/ And bleat the one at th' other," and we become aware of a world in which time moves cyclically in a process of eternal renewal.[1] To take another instance from the same episode: "Have you thought," Camillo asks Florizel, resolved for flight, "on/ A place whereto you'll go?" "Not any yet," the boy replies:

> But as th'unthought-on accident is guilty
> To what we wildly do, so we profess
> Ourselves to be the slaves of chance, and flies
> Of every wind that blows;   (IV.iv.529–534)

and we remember again. We remember that Polixenes began the trouble when he decided he had to leave Sicilia because of sneaping winds that might be blowing in the court of his Bohemia; we remember that Leontes, describing with ironic accuracy the surrender of his reason to his will, declared, "I am a feather for each wind that blows" (II.ii.153); we remember that the winds carried the infant Perdita to the seacoast of Bohemia; and we recognize that inscrutably but unmistakably the winds of the world and the winds of human passion are identical, and that more perhaps than in plays of other kinds nature and man's nature are one. But on another level something else is happening: the Bohemian coast on which Perdita lands, Shakespeare and his audience know just as well as we, exists only in the poet's mind. Each of the plays calls attention to the fact that what we are experiencing is art, not life, whether by the use of such awkward playwright surrogates as Time and Gower, or the incessant allusions to stage performance, or the drama of real characters in fairy-tale gardens, or sudden changes from tragedy to comedy, or in *The Tempest* the clear implication that Prospero is in some way to be thought of as analogous to the author of the play. A critic may take these hints and discuss the "romances" as autobiographical or as reflections on "the idea of the play," or he may essentially ignore the hints and analyze their illusory worlds in the more conventional terms they demand with equal urgency.

Whichever tack he takes, the critic who treats the plays thus must reduce them to one of their components. Two instances will illustrate my point. As early as 1947 Northrop Frye, pointing to the self-conscious unreality of the "world of fairies, dreams, disembodied souls, and pastoral lovers" that comprise the world of Shakespeare's comedies, noted that "the famous speech of Prospero about the dream nature of reality applies equally to Milan and the enchanted island," and argued that *The Tempest* leads us to a "detachment of the spirit born of two illusory realities." I do not want to quarrel with Frye's convincing assertion about what *The Tempest* makes us realize about the reality of the "real" world, the dream nature of our own Milans. What does call for comment, however, is the conclusion he draws: "We need not ask whether this [detachment of the spirit] brings us into a higher order of existence or not, for the question of existence is not relevant to poetry." [2] Eighteen years later, in *A Natural Perspective,* Frye continues to insist that the only true subject of the plays is their own art: "In comedy and romance the story seeks its own end instead of holding the mirror up to nature. Consequently comedy and romance are so obviously conventionalized that a serious interest in them soon leads to an interest in convention itself." [3] Thus, in *The Winter's Tale* the world we see is

the world symbolized by nature's power of renewal; it is the world we want; it is the world we hope our gods would want for us if they were worth worshiping. But it is "monstrous to our human reason," according to Paulina, and its truth "is so like an old tale that the verity of it is in strong suspicion." Such things happen in stories, not in life, and the world *The Winter's Tale* leaves us with is neither an object of knowledge nor of belief. [4]

My second instance is Frank Kermode's rightly admired introduction to *The Tempest*. If Frye argues that such reality as the romances imply leads us to a world that exists only in poetry, Kermode discusses art in *The Tempest* exclusively as an aspect of the nature dramatized by the play. The force of the play, he contends, is its exemplification of his definition of "romance": "a mode of exhibiting the action of magical and moral laws in a version of human life so selective as to obscure, for the special purpose of concentrating attention on these laws, the fact that in reality their force is intermittent and only fitfully glimpsed." [5] In this view, the arbitrary and obtrusive conventions of the romances serve to make the plays seem normative, to make us feel that because they generalize and abstract life they are realer than reality. As Frye must deny that the plays attempt to lead us out to the world, so Kermode simply dismisses the "autobiographical interpretation" according to which the plays point inward to themselves as art. [6]

Frye and Kermode are worth citing not because they are wrong but because they are on the whole so right about these plays. The polarity of art and nature is so richly embodied in *Pericles, Cymbeline, The Winter's Tale,* and *The Tempest* as to make possible full and coherent explanations of each play in terms suggesting Shakespeare's exclusive concern with the nature of art or the artifice of nature. But the simpler the explanation, the more likely it is to reduce the play to its schema. Such criticism frustrates where most it satisfies, and makes one hope with Professor Kermode that "some critic will radically alter the assumptions upon which criticism" of these plays "is at present founded." [7]

I want to suggest here that the basis for the new assumptions we need can be found in the no-man's-land so carefully skirted by Kermode and Frye, the relation between nature and art built into Shakespeare's last plays. The view of reality imposed on the audience of Shakespeare's romances has its analogues elsewhere in imaginative literature, and I propose to illuminate it by going, not like Frye to other Shakespearean comedy, or like Kermode to Renaissance speculations on nature, but rather to the final works of one of the great masters of the twentieth century, which in their technique, their subject matter, their attitude toward that matter, their tone, and their effect on an audience reveal an extraordinary affinity with Shakespeare's final plays. Thomas Mann did not call *The Holy Sinner* and *The Confessions of Felix Krull, Confidence Man* "romances"; but Shakespeare did not use the term either. What we are talking about is not a genre but a kind of art produced by a certain kind of artist at the end of a life of mastery. By looking at some points of correspondence between Mann's late novels and Shakespeare's late plays I hope to make clear a point of view from which the new kind of criticism invited by Kermode becomes possible.[8]

Written only four years before Mann's death in 1955, *The Holy Sinner* is a redaction of Hartmann von Aue's *Gregorious vom Stein*. Nothing could better illustrate its appropriateness to a consideration of Shakespeare's last plays than a brief summary of the plot. Wiligis and Sibylla, twin children of the widowed Duke of Flaundres and Artoys, consummate a sudden access of incestuous affection on the night of their father's death. Their affair produces its predictable fruit. Wiligis leaves Christian realms, entrusting his pregnant sister to the Baron Eisengrein. When her boy is born, Sibylla and the Baron's wife persuade Eisengrein to entrust him to the seas in a cask laden with assorted medieval treasures. Wiligis dies; Sibylla copes with courtship from men unacquainted with her secret; and the baby, found by fishermen on the shores of the island of Saint Dunstan, is brought to the saintly abbot Gregorius, who gives his name, abbreviated to Grigorss, to the child and finds a foster home for him with the fisherman Wiglaf and his wife Mahaute. Educated by the monk, Grigorss reaches a naturally aristocratic young manhood, instinctively chivalrous and mournful. When he is seventeen, an unsolicited fight with another of Mahaute's children leads to her angry revelation of Grigorss' mysterious arrival, and the young man leaves to seek his fortunes in the world. Even those who know neither the novel nor its source will scarcely be surprised to learn that the self-styled Knight of the Fish promptly makes his unconscious way to a duel in which he defeats one Roger the Invincible, who for years has sought the hand of Sibylla, and that the upshot is Grigorss' marriage to his own mother. After three years the couple learn the truth, and Grigorss, leaving his wife-mother-aunt with two daughters and a sermon on atonement, dons rags and leg iron, persuades a fisherman to ferry him to a bare rock at sea, and spends seventeen penitent years exposed to the elements, locked into the fetal position, nourished by a curious milk produced by the rock until he turns into a tiny hedgehoglike creature. In the last movement of the novel, a crisis occurs in the papal succession, and inspired respectively by a vision and a miracle two Romans set out to find the true successor—one Gregorius. Finding the fisherman who took Grigorss to the rock, the Romans watch as he discovers a key in the fish he is cleaning. The key, it turns out, is to the leg iron locked onto Grigorss by the fisherman seventeen years ago, and the fisherman had thrown it into the waves, swearing he would believe his odd passenger was genuinely a holy penitent only if he should see the key again. The discovery leads rapidly to the restoration of Grigorss' human form, to his investiture as Pope, and to a reunion with his penitent mother, now promoted to Abbess, and with his daughters by her, who, as Clemens points out, are the Pope's nieces; and the novel ends in a radiant mood of reconciliation and praise of God.

The complexity of Mann's romance is as rich as the impulse that turned the author of *Doctor Faustus* toward its material in his eighth decade, and I can only hint now at those elements of *The Holy Sinner* that make it impossible when reading it not to think of Shakespeare's last phase.

First of all there is the material: the outlandish saint's life—
fairy tale of familial separations, reunions, and sexual problems, baldly presented in all its absurdity, yet simultaneously
in a lovingly realized ambiance of an authentic romance
world replete with courts and tourneys, fishermen's huts and
sparkling seas, hidden bedrooms, hunts, and anachronistic
Toledo swords. It is a story hard for its own participants to
believe without faith: thus, when one of the churchmen who
find Grigorss on the rock worries about how he will be
received when he returns with a hedgehog in his bosom and
crowns it with the papal tiara, Gregorius asks him to believe
that the heaven that has nourished him on rock's milk will
certainly restore him to man's estate; and with equal ex-
plicitness the narrator requests faith of the audience as the
penitent is returned to his original condition by the sacra-
mental function of the ordinary bread and wine he eats on
the return trip. Demanding that we assent to a preposterous
story so bewitchingly narrated as frequently to move us,
Mann uses his tale to awaken us to the magical beauty of
the ordinary, the fish with its belly cut open in the hut, the
crowds in the streets of Rome, the love of man and woman.
Grigorss' rebirth is absurd and tongue-in-cheek yet deeply
affecting; parallel to his earlier "birth out of the wild waves,"[9]
it reminds us as well of Joseph's rebirth from the well into
which he had been cast, which almost two decades earlier
Mann had detailed with a similar implication of the spiritual
rebirth that is the central experience of all lives worth cele-
brating—those that William James called the "twice-born."
As in Shakespeare's last plays, then, a self-consciously primi-
tive narrative serves to provide an experience simultaneously

entertaining and evocative of the self's inner life, and does so by making us regard its material all at once as mere story-telling and realer than life itself.

The virtuosity and charm of the narrative do not alone account for the excitement it arouses. At least as important is the sense Mann gives of the force that drives the events of the story. In the world of *The Holy Sinner* every event has three causes. To Wiligis, to Sibylla, to Grigorss, the action is a sequence of disasters apparently unmitigated until the end, but their medium is a plot in which each disaster proves to be part of a providential scheme. Life for the novel's characters has some of the qualities of a dream, in which circumstances move toward unforeseen but inevitable ends and the dreamer knows least the meaning of his own actions. Grigorss' sin is the foundation of his blessing; we shall learn later that at the crucial moment he knows deeply that he is committing an act of incest, yet watching him at that moment we see him so out of touch with the realities of his inner life that in a more crucial sense he does not know what he is doing. Such a welter of knowing and not knowing, sinning yet helplessness before impulses not of their own making, of suicidal steps toward their ultimate rebirth touches the characterization of Prospero, Pericles, and Leontes. Even the fisherman's angry toss of the key turns out to be a providential act which leads to the discovery of the penitent, who, it turns out, has grown small enough anyway to have slipped out of the leg iron in which his antagonist had thought to imprison him. Thus two causes, one in the motions of the spirit and the other in the motions of the world, turn out to be identical.

But I said *three* causes. The third is the narrator, and here the analogy to Shakespeare is most striking. As God controls the world represented, so Clemens tells us he controls the story. At the beginning the bells of Rome are ringing wildly. At the end we will learn that the occasion of their ringing is the three-day coronation of Pope Gregory, from which point the garrulous narrator looks back to the story's beginning. Who rings the bells? he asks at the outset, and well he might: the bell-ringers have run into the street to see the new pope, the ropes hang slack. The ringing of the bells is a miracle, like the other miracles that have brought Grigorss to his final glory, additional proof of the operation of God's grace in the world. But Clemens has another answer to his question:

Who is ringing the bells? . . . . Shall one say that *nobody* rings them? No, only an ungrammatical head, without logic, would be capable of the utterance. "The bells are ringing": that means they are rung, and let the bell-chambers be never so empty.—So who is ringing the bells of Rome?—*It is the spirit of story-telling.* . . . He it is that says: "All the bells were ringing"; and, in consequence, it is he who rings them. So spiritual is this spirit, and so abstract that grammatically he can be talked of only in the third person and simply referred to as "It is he." And yet he can gather himself into a person, namely into the first person, and be incarnate in somebody who speaks in him and says: "I am he. I am the spirit of story-telling, who, sitting in his time place, namely in the library of the cloister of St. Gall in Allemannenland, . . . tells this story for entertainment and exceptional edification; in that I begin with its grace-abounding end and ring the bells of Rome: *id est,* report that on that day of processional entry they all together began to ring of themselves.   (pp. 4–5; italics Mann's)

Who rings the bells? Who chooses the "chosen" of Mann's German title, *Der Erwählte?* Providence does; the narrator does: there is no distinction.

Three years earlier Mann had focused *Doctor Faustus* on its narrator as well as its hero; in *The Holy Sinner* the split focus is even more important. As we respond to the events of the real world projected by the narrative, we repeatedly find the narrator calling attention to his role; God's manipulation of that world is identical to the storyteller's manipulation of the plot. Let me cite two characteristic moments. "Now behold how God brought it to pass, and with the utmost dexterity contrived against Himself, that the Lord Grimald's grandson, the child of the bad children, should come happily to shore in a cask." [10] We need hardly have noticed that earlier Clemens had taken credit for imagining the loading of the cask himself (p. 68) to see the implication that the life which is the subject of the plot is a work of art contrived by God, a comedy, even a joke in which at the end the new pope can meet his ex-wife and call her "mother" and she with equal accuracy can call him "Father." The second instance is an apotheosis. In that final scene, Grigorss and Sibylla confess what we have long suspected: when they broke the taboo, each of them was darkly aware of what he was doing: in pretending to be simply lovers, they "play-acted," Grigorss says, [11]—ironically the interview occurs in a chapter entitled "The Audience"—and later: "We thought to offer God an entertainment." [12]

Life as an entertainment for God! This, I propose, is the vision of the romances. It explains the otherwise inexplicable insistence in the plays that the life presented as a version of our lives is itself like art, the insistence that as people who act we are like actors in a play, the haunting analogies between Prospero's mastery and Shakespeare's, the simultaneous presentation of irremediable evil in a context in which grace triumphs and the potency of evil becomes itself part of a beautiful landscape, a spectacle to amuse us as well as an image of our lives' reality.

> Go play, boy, play. Thy mother plays, and I
> Play too, but so disgraced a part, whose issue
> Will hiss me to my grave,

says Leontes, and later Hermione, defending herself against a grief that is "more/ Than history can pattern, though devised/ And played to take spectators," rightly guesses that because "powers divine/ Behold our human actions," her play must have a happy ending. "The dignity of this act was worth the audience of kings and princes, for by such was it acted."

> Good Paulina,
> Lead us from hence, where we may leisurely
> Each one demand and answer to his part
> Performed in this wide gap of time since first
> We were dissevered.[13]

"We thought to offer God an entertainment."

"How inventive life is! Lending substance to airy nothings, it brings our childhood dreams to pass." Neither a comment on Prospero's farewell to his art nor a passage from *The Holy Sinner,* that remark is made by Felix Krull as he contemplates his successful parlaying of a Parisian waiter's role into his triumphant assumption of the name and fortunes of the Marquis de Venosta.[14] Begun in 1911, laid down as if forever, resumed only a year before Mann's death without the slightest flicker of a change in tone, *The Confessions of Felix Krull* spans a virtual lifetime of obsession with the artist's role. In what may turn out to be the comic masterpiece of the twentieth century, Mann plays on the theme of art and life a set of variations which could justify a good deal of analysis, and I shall merely indicate schematically some of the novel's features that, taken with what I have been observing at greater length in *The Holy Sinner,* point to a new perspective on Shakespeare's romances.

A parodic version of Mann's earlier Joseph, making his miraculous way through an unmiraculous world by a combination of comic shrewdness, protean ability to transform himself in a never-ending series of impostures, and an unfailing luck that seems somehow complementary to his own capacities, Felix Krull is the last and most complex of his author's artist-heroes. His resemblance to Shakespeare's Autolycus is nothing less than astonishing. Both men glory in an amoral mastery of the raw materials of life by force of their artistry as well as in their outrageous yet delightful playing on the weaknesses of all those who become grist for their mill. "My father named me Autolycus," boasts Shakespeare's confidence man, "who being, as I am, littered under Mercury, was likewise a snapper-up of unconsidered trifles" (IV. iii. 24–26); and if the genealogy puts us in mind of Odysseus, son of another Autolycus, as still another analogue to a hero who triumphs repeatedly over a comic world through a constantly self-transforming wit, it points more significantly at an identification with Hermes, patron alike of artists and thieves.

Introducing him at a tender age to the world of classical antiquity, Krull's godfather, Schimmelpreester, had cited the case of Phidias to teach him the identity of artist and thief,[15] and the ready student had promptly realized the appropriateness of the lesson in his first encounter with the shabbiness that hides backstage behind the illusion of the theater. Putting his lesson to work, young Krull pretends to be sick so that he may stay home from school:

I had produced these symptoms as effectively as though I had nothing to do with their appearance. I had improved upon nature, realized a dream; and only he who has succeeded in creating a compelling and effective reality out of nothing, out of sheer inward knowledge and contemplation—in short out of nothing more than imagination and the daring exploitation of his own body—he alone understands the strange and dreamlike satisfaction with which I rested from my creative task. (p. 36)

Even now he further combines the roles of artist and thief by satisfying the hunger to which a solicitous physician has condemned him by eating stolen chocolates. But under the tutelage of another kind of teacher he learns his true role in Greek mythology. Having stolen a jewel case from a wealthy traveler at the customs office on the French border, Krull meets her again in his tenure as elevator boy at the Hotel St. James and Albany in Paris where, calling himself Armand, he becomes her lover:

"You call me 'dear child'?" she cried, embracing me stormily and burying her mouth in my neck. "Oh, that's delicious! That's much better than 'sweet whore'! That's a much deeper delight than anything you've done, you artist in love. A little naked liftboy lies beside me, and calls me 'dear child,' me, Diane Philibert! *C'est exquis, ça me transporte! Armand, chéri,* I didn't mean to offend you. I didn't mean to say that you're especially stupid. All beauty is stupid because it simply exists as an object for glorification by the spirit. Let me see you, see you completely —heaven help me, how beautiful you are! The breast so sweet in its smooth, clear strength, the slim arms, the noble ribs, the narrow hips, and, oh, the Hermes legs—"

"Stop it, Diane, this isn't right. It is I who should be praising you."

"Nonsense! That's just a male convention. We women are lucky that our curves please you. But the divine, the masterpiece of creation, the model of beauty, that's you, you young, very young men with Hermes legs. Do you know who Hermes is?"

"I must admit at the moment—"

"*Céleste!* Diane Philibert is making love with someone who has never heard of Hermes! What a delicious degradation of the spirit! I will tell you, sweet fool, who Hermes is. He is the suave god of thieves." (p. 175)

Only now does Krull confess the theft of her jewelry, and her response caps one of the novel's funniest scenes: the soldier of fortune playing elevator boy must now devote his artistry to the role of thief in the acting out of Diane's favorite fantasy: while she pretends to lie asleep, he must steal her jewelry.

Like Autolycus, Krull combines Hermes' two roles in one, the confidence man, who uses his powers of transformation to turn his audiences into his victims. Thus, in his preinduction physical examination Krull plays the role of an eager would-be soldier afflicted by epilepsy: like the artist that he is, he creates an illusion so potent that his medical audience, their interest kindled by the performance, must interpret every detail as a clue to a meaning which they can elucidate with critical superiority. For the confidence man, artistry is heroism; the creative ego asserts its force, whether in loving or in stealing, by transforming nature. The artist assumes his roles both to participate in life and to master it.

Autolycus' amoral mastery, we remember, adorns the fertility rites of *The Winter's Tale,* and the complexity of Shakespeare's vision refuses to allow us to separate the rogue from other aspects of art with which the play is concerned. Consider one sequence. Pretending to have been beaten and robbed so that he can pick the Clown's pocket, Autolycus announces that he will follow his victim to the festivities where he will add a new meaning to sheep-shearing by fleecing the shearers. As he leaves the stage singing an innocent ballad about the merry heart (most of his ballads are about transformation), the action moves to the ceremony. There immediately Florizel quiets Perdita's uneasiness about the propriety of playing the role of queen of the festival by observing that the gods themselves transform themselves, taking on human shapes. Now Perdita, the princess cast by life in the role of shepherdess, plays the queen of curds and cream while Polixenes suddenly assumes the frightening role Leontes had played in the comedy's tragic half. As she describes the herbs and flowers she hands round they become natural symbols of the life represented in the play—of life renewed in the winter, of grace and remembrance—as if they were nature's own art; and when Perdita rejects hybrid flowers because art has abetted nature in producing them, Polixenes replies conclusively that the art that mends nature is itself the product of nature. Or, as Autolycus puts it in another key, "Sure the gods do this year connive at us, and we may do any thing extempore" (IV.iv.664–665).

That is Mann's point. The sheep-shearing of *The Confessions of Felix Krull* is the sequence in which the hero, disguised as the Marquis de Venosta, listens with fascination to Professor Kuckuck's discourse on life in the dining car of a train bound for Lisbon, and then, arrived at Lisbon, visits the Professor's Museum of Natural History. Like Prospero's island the museum is an image of both art and nature, and there Krull comes to terms with the underlying thematic principle of the novel: man, occupant of a tiny corner of space and time, is yet the grand climax of all nature's designs, and Krull, confidence man and player of roles, is nature's end, its final product: "All this inspired in me the moving reflection that these first beginnings, however absurd and lacking in dignity and usefulness, were preliminary moves in the direction of me—that is, of Man; and this it was that prompted my attitude of courteous self-possession as I was introduced to a marine saurian, a bare-skinned, sharp-jawed creature, represented by a five-metre-long model floating in a glass tank" (p. 301). The comic argument demonstrated in the ensuing episodes is that the force that created the universe and put it into motion in time, into perpetual metamorphosis, is identical to the force that moves Krull to the creation of his artistic hegemony, his seduction of Zouzou Kuckuck, and his joyous account of his own exploits.

What makes that account comic is what in other kinds of literature produces exactly the opposite effect: the centrality of ego in art and nature. That perception produces the ultimate irony of *The Confessions:* the hero who is artist of his own life is also the narrator, the artist who turns the materials of his experience into the art that we experience. Only such a confidence man's trick can permit Mann to convey the almost inexpressible vision that controls the novel, in which life itself comes to seem like a work of art. Mann shares his vision with the Shakespeare of the romances, and it should thus be no surprise that in them Shakespeare takes pains to remind us ever that what we are watching is both life and art, reality and dream.[16] Nor should we any longer be embarrassed by the autobiographical implications of Prospero. For Shakespeare's point in creating a protagonist who is both playwright and player and in unmistakably reminding us of his own career is not to make the audience think of him, but rather to make it see that the artist is himself the most potent image of the human condition as these works have been portraying it.

If Shakespeare reminds us in his last plays of the Renaissance commonplace that the artist is a second God creating a second nature, he does so in order to share a more profound perception that God has created our universe as a work of art. Seen from the point of view common to the romances we have considered, art and life are one. "Your actions are my dreams,"[17] says Leontes to Hermione in a profoundly ironic moment—ironic because on one level of our awareness his jealousy is only a matter of his dreams, on another because so much in the play is called dream at one point or another that all its objective reality comes to seem like a dream to its participants, and finally because the play itself is our dream of wish-fulfillment, a transformation of the art of tragedy into the life of comedy. "What is called fate," Felix Krull observes, "is actually ourselves, working through unknown but infallible laws" (p. 119). Subject and object merge in the self seen as a player of roles in a plot whose outcome and meaning are determined by a coalition between ego and providence that leads always to poetic justice. If such justice requires that we be aware of moral law, the moral implications of the hero's actions ultimately matter less than their quality as spectacle. Every motion of the spirit, every event of life, is infinitely serious, yet, as such stuff as dreams are made on, as an inconsequential ripple on the flux of time, infinitely trivial, the subject of an entertainment for a play's audience constantly reminded it is an audience, and for the gods.

BARBARA K. LEWALSKI

Milton:
Revaluations
of Romance

ALTHOUGH MILTON DID NOT WRITE romances, he formulated definite ideas about this literary kind and frequently used elements of romance in his poems. The fit audience Milton sought will recognize readily enough that he understood, loved, and responded imaginatively to a wide variety of works in the romance mode—*The Squire's Tale, Morte d'Arthur,* the Italian Romantic epics, *The Faerie Queene*[1]— eschewing the fashionable contemporary denigrations of them. The fit audience should perceive also that the romance materials used so extensively in Milton's poems serve primarily to redefine and to revalue the themes, motifs, and attitudes characteristic of this mode.

Romantic epics were denounced by some Italian neo-Aristotelian critics on the ground that their multiple plots violated the unity of action essential to the heroic poem and that their marvels and wonders violated the canon of probability.[2] Though Milton was a classicist who constructed unified plots, in his *Reason of Church Government* (1642) he echoes the argument of Ariosto's defenders[3] as he queries whether, in epic, "the rules of *Aristotle* herein are strictly to be kept, or nature to be follow'd, which in them that know art, and use judgement, is no transgression, but an inriching of art." [4]

Another popular complaint about romances, reiterated by sober-minded English Protestants from Roger Ascham to Henry Vaughan, characterized them as lewd and lascivious fictions which supplanted the true stories of the Bible in men's minds and promoted wantonness.[5] Milton held no brief for this position. Once, in *Eikonoklastes* (1649), he invited these stock Puritan responses by referring to "the polluted orts and refuse of *Arcadia's* and *Romances*,"[6] but the context limits the application of that comment specifically to the close paraphrase of the pagan Pamela's prayer from Sidney's *Arcadia,* which is incorporated in the *Eikon Basilike* as one of King Charles' prayers to the living God composed while he awaited execution. Such blasphemous uses of romance aside, Milton can refer in the same tract to the *Arcadia* as "a Book in that kind full of worth and witt."[7] Here, as earlier in his *Apology for Smectymnuus* (1642), romances are judged according to the cardinal Miltonic principle that the nature of the reader rather than the matter of the books determines whether they will promote vice or virtue. More than this, the *Apology* reveals Milton's conception of romance as setting forth a golden world with heroes who, like Spenser's heroes, are ideal images of virtue. He is not so far from Northrop Frye's description of romance as a mode whose organizing ideas are "chastity and magic."[8] Describing where his younger feet trod, Milton declared,

I betook me among those lofty Fables and Romances. . . . There I read it in the oath of every Knight, that he should defend to the expence of his best blood, or of his life, if it so befell him, the honour and chastity of Virgin or Matron. From whence even then I learnt what a noble vertue chastity sure must be, to the defence of which so many worthies by such a deare adventure of themselves had sworne. And if I found in the story afterward any of them by word or deed breaking that oath, I judg'd it the same fault of the Poet, as that which is attributed to *Homer;* to have written undecent things of the gods.[9]

The other stock objection to romances, widely diffused

in criticism influenced by Christian Platonism, condemned them as lying fables, extravagant fictions, having no relation to truth.[10] Milton understood that fiction is of the essence of romance: his constant synonyms for this mode are "fable" and "feigning." These terms in themselves have no pejorative connotations, however, as Milton describes his youthful wanderings "among those lofty Fables and Romances," or observes that Satan's forces outnumbered "what resounds / In Fable or *Romance*" about King Arthur's forces, or refers to events in particular works with the phrase "As Spenser (or Ariosto) feigns."[11] Nor did he object to supernatural marvels, magic, or exotic wonders. *Il Penseroso*'s speaker takes delight in the marvels of *The Squire's Tale*—"The vertuous Ring and Glass" and "the wondrous Hors of Brass" —and lovingly evokes the special romance mood of wonderful knightly feats and exotic landscapes:

And if aught else, great Bards beside
In sage and solemn tunes have sung,
Of Tourneys and of Trophies hung,
Of Forests, and enchantments drear,
Where more is meant than meets the ear.   (ll. 116–120)

The last line suggests that romance-feigning and wonders may convey moral and allegorical truth, for Milton the chief value to be found in such works. Because Spenser teaches moral virtue allegorically—for example, "true temperance under the person of *Guion*"—Milton praises him as a better teacher even than Scotus or Aquinas.[12] Moreover, Milton's references in his *Commonplace Book* to Boiardo,

Ariosto, and Tasso on such subjects as lying, almsgiving, and slander indicate that, although their works are not continuous allegories, they nevertheless convey moral truth through precept, sentence, and exemplum.[13]

A Masque Presented at Ludlow Castle is Milton's closest approach to romance considered as a feigned story which teaches moral truth through allegory. It presents a version of the romance quest with the classic three-part structure defined by Frye—the perilous journey, the crucial struggle, the exaltation of the hero.[14] It frequently echoes situations, motifs, and language from romance, especially from Spenser. Comus and his rout derive from the Circe episode in the *Odyssey* via Alcina's Garden, Armida's Garden, and especially Acrasia's Bower of Bliss.[15] The Lady immobilized in her chair by Comus recalls Amoret chained and tormented by Busirane in the Masque of Cupid.[16] The Lady lost in the "blind mazes of this tangl'd Wood" (l. 182) and deceived by the disguised Comus recalls Spenser's Wandering Wood and the deception of Red Cross and Una by the disguised Archimago.[17] Sabrina, whose story is told in the *Faerie Queene,* recalls such ladies as Ariosto's Melissa, whose magical powers dispel evil enchantments and free enthralled knights.[18]

Yet Milton's dominant concern with the moral truth to be conveyed prevents him from developing his Ludlow Masque in the romance mode. His fiction has not in itself the importance and value of Spenser's fiction, but is thoroughly subordinated to the allegory. And the romance allusions redefine the heroism of the Spenserian romance quest in terms which are truer to what Milton sees as the realities of the human condition. At first the Elder Brother speaks of his sister as something of a knight of chastity, fully armored against all harm and able to meet any adventure in whatever perilous romance landscape she might find herself:

> 'Tis chastity, my brother, chastity:
> She that has that, is clad in complete steel,
> And like a quiver'd Nymph with Arrows keen
> May trace huge Forests and unharbor'd Heaths,
> Infamous Hills and sandy perilous wilds, . . .
> Yea there, where very desolation dwells,
> By grots and caverns shagg'd with horrid shades,
> She may pass on with unblench't majesty.   (ll. 420–430)

But the Lady is no Britomart or Bradamante with enchanted spear, able to overthrow all enemies, no Diana or Belphoebe capable of dispatching offensive Actaeons or lustful giants, no unconquerable Galahad who can restore the Wasteland. Nor, on the other hand, is she a helpless Amoret suffering mental anguish and a tormented bleeding heart at the hands of her courtly love captor; the Lady says, rightly, "Thou canst not touch the freedom of my mind / With all thy charms" (ll. 663–664). She is more like Spenser's Una—in need of protection, though possessed of a strength of her own. Una, however, in her adventure with the fawns and satyrs of the woods, "astonied" and tamed that "rude, mis-shapen, monstrous rabblement," [19] whereas the Lady has no power over Comus' rabble rout and her goodness amazes Comus only momentarily. The Brothers, though possessed of the moly of Temperance and the advice of the Attendant Spirit, cannot capture Comus as Guyon with his Palmer captured Acrasia, nor can they, like Britomart with Busirane, force him to reverse his spell. He escapes, and will continue to occupy the wood.

In the dark wood, the condition of fallen nature, Virtue protects the Lady's spiritual integrity. Her mind is not attracted to bestial intemperance. Her physical body, however, is subject to the forces of disordered nature and sensuality represented by Comus; she cannot be released from them through her virtue, or by any human agency. Still less can she alter these conditions of life. When Sabrina (heavenly grace) frees her and makes possible the children's continued journey to their father's house, the Attendant Spirit warns that the woods and Comus threaten still:

> Come Lady, while Heaven lends us grace,
> Let us fly this cursed place,
> Lest the Sorcerer us entice
> With some other new device.   (ll. 938–941)

The Spirit presents the children to their parents as if they have achieved a romance quest:

> Heav'n hath timely tri'd their youth,
> Their faith, their patience, and their truth,
> And sent them here through hard assays
> With a crown of deathlesse Praise,
>   To triumph in victorious dance
>   O're sensual Folly and Intemperance.   (ll. 970–975)

The children have accomplished a perilous journey, but in a world where the quests of knights-errant to prove their virtue or to rid the land of evils are inappropriate;[20] the trials and tests are sent by heaven. The Lady has engaged in a crucial struggle with Comus, but without effecting the death or clear defeat of the evil power; her victory is simply the preservation of her spiritual freedom. The exaltation of the children is not for heroic deeds done, but for manifesting in the dark wood "Their faith, their patience, and their truth." [21] Whereas Spenser had emphasized the power of Virtue to overwhelm Vice and reclaim the erring, so that the actual and the ideal, Britain and Faeryland, could be coextensive, Milton rather emphasizes the freedom Virtue brings—to resist spiritual thralldom, and ultimately to climb "Higher than the Sphery chime" (aided, as need be, by heaven). In *A Masque* the images of partially restored nature (the masque dances at Ludlow Castle, the Happy Gardens to which the Spirit flies)[22] are set off sharply from the fallen world; a hero may attain them after enduring the trials sent in the dark wood, but he can hardly hope to extend their boundaries.

In spite of Milton's theoretical acceptance of romance-feigning, his concern with moral truth in the Ludlow Masque kept him from conceiving that work as a romance. For epic poetry he rejected romance fictions in theory as well as in practice, agreeing with Tasso that the heroic poem should be grounded upon historical truth. His early speculations casting Arthur in the role of English epic hero assume his historicity: the *Commonplace Book* cites information about Arthur and his Round Table from John Hardying's *Chronicle;* in *Mansus* (1638–39) Milton proposes "to summon back our native kings into our songs, and Arthur" and "to proclaim the magnanimous heroes of the table which their mutual fidelity made invincible." [23] However, when he studied the sources systematically in 1648–49 for his *History of Britain*,[24] Milton evidently became disabused about the historical Arthur, and in that work disavows him with all the truculence of one who has been deceived on a matter of importance. Arthur was "more renown'd in Songs and Romances, then in true stories"; chroniclers who write of him, "quickly swell a volume with trash," and readers who believe in him are such as "can accept of Legends for good story." [25] Among the factors that brought Milton to the epic subject that pleased him, "long chusing and beginning late," one was certainly the discovery that Arthur was a subject fit for the fabling of romances rather than the truth of epic.

In the Proem to Book IX of *Paradise Lost* Milton formally undertakes to surpass all other heroic poems, epic or romance. The argument of his poem is "not less but more Heroic" than the arguments of classical epics, though it renounces the accepted epic-romance subject—"Wars, hitherto the only Argument / Heroic deem'd." He contemns romance fiction specifically, as unworthy the noble endeavor of epic: "to dissect / With long and tedious havoc fabl'd Knights / In Battles feign'd." He also disparages the conventional apparatus of epic, and especially of romance, as affording no appropriate basis for determining what a heroic poem is:

> to describe Races and Games,
> Or tilting Furniture, emblazon'd Shields,
> Impreses quaint, Caparisons, and Steeds;

Bases and tinsel Trappings, gorgeous Knights
At Joust and Tournament; then marshall'd Feast
Serv'd up in Hall with Sewers, and Senaschals;
The Skill of Artifice or Office mean,
Not that which justly gives Heroic name
To Person or to Poem.   (IX.33–41)

Milton claims the title of heroic poet solely by reason of the
height and truth of his argument and the answerable style
the celestial patroness will bring. Having made this clear, he
can lay under contribution most of the great epic poetry of
the past, and to a lesser but significant extent, romance as well.
For example, the allegorical figures of Sin and Death, despite
their classical and medieval lineage, derive most immediately
from Spenser (Sin might almost be the archetype of Duessa).
And Milton's Paradise of Fools is a more sharply satiric re-
working of Ariosto's Lunar Valley whither Orlando's lost
wits strayed.[26]

Much more interesting is Milton's use of that central
romance situation, the pleasure garden inhabited by lovers.
Since his Eden is well-nigh unique among theological and
literary conceptions of Eden in being a Garden of Love
where a pair of idyllic lovers enjoy each other in their blissful
Bower, the romance tradition is especially relevant.[27] Many
gardens from romantic epics—for example Alcina's,
Armida's, and Acrasia's—are emblems of the moral enerva-
tion caused by wanton indulgence in pleasure; the Lady of
the Garden enthralls her knight-lovers, keeping them from
their vocations of mighty conquest. Another variety of romance garden is Spenser's Garden of Adonis, where joyful
lovers freely and frankly take their pleasure of each other in

a static and cyclical order whose great purposes are generation, natural fruition, and natural joy.

Milton designed his romance garden as a counterpoint to these paradigms, and in the process revalued romance conceptions of love.[28] At Adam and Eve's first appearance their sensual delight in each other—"Imparadis't in one another's arms"—is clearly evident to the reader and to the jealous Satan, but here Adam's proper hierarchical superiority is maintained in the love relationship. One of the challenges laid upon Adam is precisely to live in and to enjoy the most perfect and pleasurable Garden of Love ever known without becoming enervated by pleasure or in any degree enthralled by the wife-mistress who is the epitome of the garden's delights. Adam meets other challenges as well, since in Milton's garden there are ends besides natural pleasure and generation. Day by day Adam and Eve must dress and keep the garden, clearing the "Alleys . . . with branches overgrown," and pruning the branches of their "wanton growth," thereby assuming responsibility for the continued creative ordering of their world.[29] They must cope with a tremendous knowledge explosion, assimilating at great speed a mass of new experiences and new information about the natural world, about angelic wars and the theology of creation and cosmological theory, and about themselves. They must also be in constant readiness for the great combat with Evil which is to occur within (not outside of) the Garden of Love. And all of this they are to accomplish with due proportion and without undue anxiety, constantly enjoying and enhancing their love. Adam does not stand up to these challenges, but they are conditions no romance lover has ever encountered. Clearly Milton cannot view the Edenic Garden of Love as preparation for, or as respite from, moral trial and responsibility: its pleasures are inextricably bound up with the complexities and challenges and tensions of responsible moral life. To meet the task Adam is set in his Garden of Love would be something of a heroic achievement: the attainment of a fully human life and love in the State of Innocence.

The episode of the Fall has as one of its dimensions the decline from this revalued ideal of love into conventional romantic attitudes. Eve assumes the faulty heroism of a knight-errant looking for adventures to prove her unaided virtue, whereas in the Edenic world as in the dark wood these are foolish attitudes: "Trial will come unsought" (IX.366), and human virtue has need of aid to sustain itself. Adam knows better, knows that "tender love enjoins, / That I should mind thee oft, and mind thou me" (IX.357–358).[30] Satan plays upon Eve's self-image as heroine, insinuating to her that she should prove her "dauntless virtue" (IX.694) by daring the death threatened by God in the adventure of the Tree. At his Fall, Adam places the incident in the same context: "Bold deed thou hast presum'd, advent'rous *Eve*" (IX.921). More important, Satan approaches Eve separated from Adam as a courtly lover, inviting her by his extravagant flattery to regard herself as a conventional romance Lady, goddess to her lovers and elevated far above them. In deciding instantly to share Eve's fate, Adam becomes a romantic lover, a Lancelot who places service to his lady above all other ends and would gladly die at her command. Eve praises his action as just such a romance gesture, a "glorious trial of exceeding Love" (IX.961).

In the Ludlow Masque the romance allusions and motifs revalue romance ideals of heroism by displaying how the conditions of the fallen world limit the power of heroic virtue. In *Paradise Lost* such allusions serve chiefly to revalue the conventional romantic idea of Love by measuring it against the more perfect ideal defined in the Edenic world. In Milton's brief epic, *Paradise Regained,* the romance allusions have another function: to suggest that Jesus' adventure and conquest over Satan in the Wilderness is the true, fully achieved Romance Quest; that, as Jesus echoes, fulfills, and surpasses heroes from biblical and classical history and myth, so does he also antitype the romance knights; and that the wonders of his story are greater than romance marvels. Accordingly, the Parthian forces displayed before Christ far outnumber the great armies of pagan and Christian knights gathered "When *Agrican* with all his Northern powers / Besieg'd *Albracca,* as Romances tell." [31] And Satan, transporting Jesus to the Tower "without wing / of *Hippogrif,*" [32] effects a marvel surpassing Astolfo's flight on Ariosto's fabulous beast.

For this poem Malory's *Morte d'Arthur* and especially the story of the Grail quest, with its wildernesses, storms, and various disguisings of the fiend, provides the most signficant romance context. The banquet scene, with its range of sensory delights—all food and drinks, music and odors, youths and nymphs—has numerous literary sources, among them Armida's banquet in Tasso's *Gerusalemme Liberata,* [33] but the influence of Malory is pointed by an explicit allusion. The lovely ladies in the grove were "Fairer than feign'd of old, or fabl'd since / Of Fairy Damsels met in Forest wide / By Knights of *Logres,* or of *Lyones,* / *Lancelot* or *Pelleas,* or *Pellenore*" (II.358–361). Like Jesus, these later knights-errant undertake quests in forests and wildernesses, but like the first Adam they prove susceptible in some degree to sensory delight and especially to the allurements of women. Lancelot, besotted by wine, slept twice with the fair Elaine, thinking her to be Guinevere; also, though he repented his sins, his passion for Guinevere prevented his achievement of the Grail quest.[34] Pelleas was so violently in love with the scornful Ettard that he submitted to all manner of despiteful and degrading treatment from her.[35] Pellenore's son Percivale, probably alluded to here under his father's name, endured during the grail-quest a three-day fast in the wilderness, after which a lady warned him that he was apt to "die in this rock for pure hunger, and be eaten with wild beasts." She then presented him with a banquet having "all manner of meats that he could think on," and "the strongest wine that ever he drank." Stimulated by the food and drink, he urged the lady to lie with him, and was saved from serious sin only by a chance sign of the cross which caused the pavillion to vanish, and the lady to be revealed at length as "the master fiend of hell."[36]

Jesus achieves, as Adam did not and as fallen man cannot, the highest romance purposes: he is not deflected from his quest by romance ladies in groves and bowers, and he wins, by his virtue and the Divine Power, a decisive victory over Evil which significantly alters the human condition. He defeats and overwhelms the Tempter who "Fell whence he stood to see his Victor fall" (IV.571), exactly as a hero of epic or romance ought to do, though of course the wound inflicted is not physical, the heroic action is the passion of patience and heroic martydom, and the full dimensions of the victory are yet to be realized. Like *Paradise Lost, Paradise Regained* is conceived as a heroic poem grounded upon a true event; it is not a romance.[37] In the brief epic, however, the romance allusions do not revalue the romance ethos so much as exalt it to the order of perfection.

Notes

Notes

NOTES TO MALORY AND ROMANCE

BY HELAINE NEWSTEAD

1. The range is illustrated in *A Manual of the Writings in Middle English, 1050–1500,* fascicule I, ed. J. B. Severs (New Haven: Connecticut Academy of Arts and Sciences, 1967). See also O. Kratins, *PMLA,* LXXXI (1966), 347–355.

2. E. Auerbach, *Mimesis,* trans. W. Trask (Princeton: Princeton University Press, 1953), pp. 122–142.

3. *Ibid.,* p. 140.

4. For example, Northrop Frye, *Anatomy of Criticism,* (Princeton: Princeton University Press, 1957), s.v. Romance.

5. *The Vulgate Version of the Arthurian Romances,* ed. H. O. Sommer (Washington: The Carnegie Institution of Washington, 1908–1916), VI; *La Queste del Saint Graal,* ed. A. Pauphilet (Paris: Librairie Ancienne Honoré Champion, 1923); *La Mort le Roi Artu,* ed. J. Frappier (Geneva: Librairie Droz; Lille: Librairie Giard, 1954).

6. Geoffrey of Monmouth, *Historia Regum Britanniae,* ed. A. Griscom (New York: Longmans, Green, 1929); J. S. P. Tatlock, *The Legendary History of Britain* (Berkeley and Los Angeles: University of California Press, 1950); *Arthurian Literature in the Middle Ages,* ed. R. S. Loomis (Oxford: Clarendon Press, 1959), pp. 72–94.

7. Wace, *Le Roman de Brut,* 2 vols., ed. I. Arnold (Paris: Societé des Anciens Textes Français [SATF], 1939, 1940); *Arthurian Literature in the Middle Ages,* ed. Loomis, pp. 94–103.

8. *Layamon's Brut,* ed. F. Madden, 3 vols. (London, 1847); *Selections from Layamon's Brut,* ed. G. L. Brook (Oxford: Clarendon Press, 1963).

9. Tatlock, *Legendary History of Britain,* pp. 523–524; *Arthurian Literature in the Middle Ages,* ed. Loomis, pp. 107–108.

10. Layamon, ed. Madden, III, 144–145; *Selections,* ed. Brook, p. 118.

11. *Morte Arthure,* ed. E. Björkman (Heidelberg: Carl Winters; New York: G. E. Stechert, 1915). All references are cited from this edition. See also *Morte Arthure,* ed. J. Finlayson (London: Edward Arnold, 1967): long extracts with commentary.

12. W. Matthews, *The Tragedy of Arthur* (Berkeley and Los Angeles: University of California Press, 1960), pp. 33–67; *Arthurian Literature in the Middle Ages,* ed. Loomis, pp. 521–526.

13. *La Mort le Roi Artu,* ed. Frappier, pp. 226–228; J. Frappier, *Etude sur La Mort le Roi Artu* (Geneva: Librairie Droz; Paris: Librairie Minard, 1961), pp. 258–288.

14. *The Works of Sir Thomas Malory,* ed. E. Vinaver, 2nd. ed., 3 vols. (Oxford: Clarendon Press, 1967), I, 181–247. On the sources, see I, li–lxiv, xciii–xcix.

15. *Ibid.,* I, lvii, lix; III, 1366–1372.

16. *Morte Arthure,* ed. Björkman, vv. 4141–4154:

> Idrous hym ansuers ernestly þareaftyre:
> "He es my fadire in faithe, forsake sall I neuer,
> He has me fosterde and fedde and my faire bretheren.
> Bot I forsake this gate, so me Gode helpe,
> And sothely all sybredyn, bot thy selfe one.
> I breke neuer his biddynge for beryn one lyfe,
> Bot euer bouxvm as beste, blethely to wyrke.
> He commande me kyndly with knyghtly wordes,
> That I schulde lelely one þe lenge and one noo lede elles;
> I sall hys commandement holde, ȝif Criste wil me thole.
> He es eldare than I, and ende sall we bothen.
> He sall ferkke before, and I sall folowe aftyre:

ʒiffe him be destaynede to dy   todaye one þis erthe,
Criste comly with crown   take kepe to hys saule!"

17. *Works*, I, lxvi–lxxiii; III, 1275–1278, 1536–1591; C. S. Lewis, "The English Prose *Morte*," in J. A. W. Bennett, ed., *Essays on Malory* (Oxford: Clarendon Press, 1963), pp. 13–14.

18. *Ibid.*, III, 1454–1455; 1484, n. 571.9–18; 1529, n.811.33, 812.5; 1601, n.1066.25.

19. E. Vinaver, *Malory* (Oxford: Clarendon Press, 1929), pp. 36–38; *Works*, III, 1295, n.38.6; 1305, n.62.36–37; 1301, n.51.3; 1325, n.99.34–35; 1326, n.100.34–101; 1328, n.105.10.

20. *Works*, III, 1278; 1600, n.1065.4 (Camelot identified with Winchester); 1601, n.1066.23 (Astolat identified with Guildford).

21. *Works*, I, 126. See III, 1337–1338, for the elaborate French version. See also I, 151, when Morgan transforms herself and her men into stone statues, and I, 52.21–23, and corresponding note, III, 1301.

22. On chivalry in Malory, see P. E. Tucker, "Chivalry in the *Morte*," in *Essays on Malory*, ed. Bennett, pp. 64–103; R. T. Davies, "The Worshipful Way in Malory," in *Patterns of Love and Courtesy*, ed. John Lawlor (London: Edward Arnold, 1966), 157–177; S. Miko, *Medium Aevum*, XXXV (1966), 211–230; P. J. Field, *Medium Aevum*, XXXVII (1968), 37–45; D. S. Brewer, ed., *Malory: The Morte Darthur* (London: Edward Arnold, 1968), pp. 23–35.

23. *Works*, I, 120. See note, III, 1336, on this passage and on Caxton's revision of the Winchester text.

24. *Works*, I, 212–217.

25. *Ibid.*, III, 1485, n.571.25–34; 1486, n. 579, 23–25; 1522, n.779. 16–18; 1527, n.804.36–805.1. See Tucker, *Essays on Malory*, ed. Bennett, pp. 73–76.

26. *Ibid.*, III, 1174.

27. *Ibid.*, III, 1184.

28. *Ibid.*, III, 1256.

29. *Ibid.*, III, 1259.

30. *Ibid.*, III, 1662, 1655.

NOTES TO SPENSER: FROM MAGIC TO MIRACLE
BY A. BARTLETT GIAMATTI

1. *Hurd's Letters on Chivalry and Romance with the Third Elizabethan Dialogue,* ed. Edith J. Morley (London: H. Frowde, 1911), pp. 113, 136, 153.

2. The gesture itself is by no means confined to the Renaissance. The reader will have already recalled the moment in *Iliad VI* when Astyanax screams at the sight of Hector's menacing plumage: "Then his beloved father laughed out, and his honoured mother, / And at once glorious Hector lifted from his head the helmet / And laid it in all its shining upon the ground" (471–473); in Book XXII, Andromache sees Hector dragged before the city; she "threw from her head the shining gear that ordered her headdress, / the diadem and the cap, and the holding band woven together, / and the circlet which Aphrodite the golden once had given her" (468–470. Richmond Lattimore translation). The single gesture unites the family; the revelation of fatherhood, which soothes the son, is paralleled by the mother's uncovering, which underscores her inadequacy to confer identity and prefaces her poignant lament for the fate of her fatherless boy. The mutual needs of fathers and sons are at the heart of the poem. Nor should we forget the Archangel Michael, emissary of another Father, who comes to Adam and Eve: "His starry Helm unbuckl'd show'd him prime / In Manhood where Youth ended" (*Paradise Lost* XI.245–246). The chilvalric romance gives Milton this helmet and the face whose perfection resides in its balance of antithetical qualities.

3. *Ludovico Ariosto, Orlando Furioso,* ed. Nicola Zingarelli (Milan: Ulrico Hoepli, 1959); unless otherwise noted, all translations are my own.

4. On a woman's face, and smile, making paradise, see Dante, *Paradiso* XV.34–36; Petrarch, *Rime* CCXCII.5–7; parodied, as usual, by Pulci, *Morgante* XV.102 and XVI.12.

5. *Boiardo, Orlando Innamorato,* ed. Francesco Foffano, 3 vols. (Milan: UTET, 1944).

6. Text taken from *Dante's Purgatorio,* trans. and commentary by John Sinclair (New York: Oxford University Press, 1961); I have arranged as verse a somewhat revised translation.

7. *Luigi Pulci, Morgante,* ed. Franca Ageno (Milan and Naples: Riccardo Ricciardi, 1955).

8. *Virgil,* ed. and trans. H. R. Fairclough, Loeb ed. (London and Cambridge, Mass., 1915; revised, 1935); text used as basis of my translation.

9. An interesting example of the greater flexibility of a "medieval" as opposed to a Renaissance poet in adapting material from powerful literary models occurs in the treatments by Chaucer and Boccaccio of the revelations of Emilia to the imprisoned Palemon and Arcite. In *Teseida* III.8–14, Emilia's appearance in the garden and her effect on the men (Arcita: "Disse fra sè: questa è di paradiso," 12) is closely modeled on Matelda's appearance to and colloquy with the pilgrim and his guide in Eden, particularly *Purgatorio* XXVIII.37–42, 61–66, 80–81. Even Palemon's reference to Venus (stanza 14) seems to derive from Dante's reference at XXVIII.64–66. Chaucer, in *The Knight's Tale,* 1033–1122, shows much more range in his resourcefulness. The account of Emelye's hair, garland and singing as an "angel hevenysshly" (1049–1055) follows *Teseida* III.8–11; but Palamon's wonderment: "I noot wher she be woman or goddesse, / But Venus is it soothly, as I gesse" (1101–1102) conflates Boccaccio with *Aeneid* I.327–329—a passage Chaucer also exploited in *Troilus and Criseyde* I, 425—and brings Vergilian revelation into the English tradition independently of Italian romances. "therewithal on knees doun he fil, / And seyde: 'Venus, if it by thy wil / You in this garden thus to transfigure / Bifore me . . .'" (1103–1106), says Palamon who by kneeling and using the language of religious transformation foreshadows Artegall at *Faerie Queene* IV.vi.22 (see below). Text used: *The Works of Geoffrey Chaucer,* ed. F. N. Robinson (Boston: Houghton Mifflin, 1957).

10. Tasso provides the clearest example of this when Tancredi unwittingly wounds mortally his beloved Clorinda, *Gerusalemme Liberata* XII.67–68. What Tancredi sees upon raising her visor is

not immediately described: rather the poet emphasizes the effect of the revelation, tragic knowledge for Tancredi, conversion for Clorinda, and only then (st. 69) describes her face.

11. The *voyeur* is privy to the *voyant*'s insight (to no avail) when Sansloy snatches away Una's veil at I.vi.4, and his "lustful eye" feeds on her beauty shining "as brightest skye." The rhyme links the two modes of sight as the gesture links the two figures. The final apotheosis of Una occurs when she has her "widow-like sad wimple throwne away" and the "glorious light of her sunshyny face" (I.xii.22–23) picks up the language of I.iii.4—framing Book I by visions of her face. The light of Heaven is also revealed by another veil falling away —the covering on Arthur's shield which falls in the fight with Orgoglio (I.viii.9) and with the Souldan (V.viii.37). The revelations of the "sunlike shield" (V.viii.41) reestablish for the reader the condition of light and knighthood to which all other lights, and knights, aspire.

12. In the Proem to Book II, stanza 5, the face of Elizabeth is by the poet "enfold / In couert vele" because of its exceeding brightness; we get versions of its splendor in the face of Belphoebe, a "heauenly pourtrait of bright Angels hew" (II.iii.22—as seen by the *voyeur* Trompart) and in the angel's face "Like Phoebus . . . [which] Diuinely shone" (II.viii.5); while reminding us of the deceptiveness of revelation, there is in Mammon's cave Philotime's face that "wondrous faire did seeme . . . But wrought by art and counterfetted shew" (II.vii.45). We learn to eschew this "counterfetted shew" and, like Arthur, see the "vertue in vaine shew" (II.ix.3), to see, with Arthur, the living and wholesome ideal in art.

13. See also *Amoretti* XIII, XXII, XXVI. Perfection through such a mix of male and female attributes is part of Spenser's, and the Renaissance's, fascination with the Hermaphrodite.

14. Elizabeth is the fixed light for the poet at I, proem 5; images of fixed stars occur at I.ii.1; VII.vi.9; see also *Epithalamium,* lines 285–291 and 409–412. Lodestar hid in clouds, at III.iv.53, and fixed star covered, II.viii.1, both images related to the recurrent figure of

the eye of Reason blinded, I.ii.5, II.iv.7, and IV.ii.5, and to instances of the face of Heaven clouded over, II.xii.34 and III.iv.13.

15. Artegall sees in Radigund's face "A miracle of natures grace" (V.v.12) but he must learn what we learned at V.iii.39, when Bragga-docchio and the False Florimel were "uncased," or what we saw in the discoveries of the faces of Duessa and Ate, (IV.i.17–19) and of Philotime (II.viii.45) and Archimago (I.iii.38): that not all revelations are benign and wholesome. Artegall must learn the hardest lesson, to distinguish. Like Arthur, he must learn when "to doubt his dazeled sight" (II.xi.40). When Arthur and Artegall gaze at each other through upraised visors, and Artegall, "touched with entire affection, nigh him drew" (V.viii.12), then Britomart's dream at Isis Church (V.vii.14), her view of Artegall in the flesh (IV.vi.26), and in the magic glass (III.ii.24) begin to take shape as Artegall becomes more Arthur's equal, more a strong but tempered lover.

16. The poem ends with a veiled woman, Nature (VII.vii.5–6), as it began with Una veiled (I.i.4); though Nature, who veiled re-sembles Venus (IV.x.41), has male traits, like Britomart, and is dazzling, like Gloriana. Like the poem, which is her glass, Nature contains all.

17. Both Rabelais, Prologue to *The First Book,* and Marino, *L'Adone,* I.10, compare their works to the Silenus. Erasmus was mainly responsible for the diffusion of the Silenus figure in the Renaissance; see, for Erasmus and Rabelais, Walter Kaiser, *Praisers of Folly, Erasmus, Rabelais, Shakespeare* (Cambridge, Mass.: Harvard University Press, 1963), especially pp. 55–60, and for the related figures of the chameleon and Proteus, A. B. Giamatti, "Proteus Unbound: Some Versions of the Sea God in the Renaissance," in *The Disciplines of Criticism,* ed. P. Demetz, T. Greene, and L. Nelson (New Haven: Yale University Press, 1968). In his *Commentary on Psalm 33,* Erasmus connects the two literary figures for truth beneath the surface: "so far I have presented but the shell of the nut, and thus you have only tasted the husk of the barley; I just showed you Silenus. If God deigns to help us, we shall now extract the kernel, expose the

fine flour, and expound Silenus"—cited in the valuable study of Peter G. Bietenholz, *History and Biography in the Works of Erasmus of Rotterdam* (Geneva: Droz, 1966), p. 24.

NOTES TO

THE HOLY SINNER AND THE CONFIDENCE MAN:
ILLUSION IN SHAKESPEARE'S ROMANCES
BY NORMAN RABKIN

1. I.ii.67–68. All Shakespeare citations are to *William Shakespeare: The Complete Works* (The Pelican Shakespeare), Baltimore: Penguin Books, 1969.

2. "The Argument of Comedy," from *English Institute Essays, 1948,* in Leonard F. Dean, ed., *Shakespeare: Modern Essays in Criticism,* rev. ed. (New York: Oxford University Press, 1967), p. 89.

3. *A Natural Perspective: The Development of Shakespearean Comedy and Romance* (New York: Harcourt, Brace & World, 1965), p. 8. In his introduction to *The Tempest* in The Pelican Shakespeare, Frye seems much more willing to talk about plays as if they have some bearing on the world they imitate.

4. P. 16. Almost persuasive. But to make his point that the real world isn't one of the play's terms, Frye must do some interesting obscuring: e.g., "The world of Leontes' jealousy does not exist at all: only the consequences of believing in it exist" (p. 115). All that it means to say that the world of Leontes' jealousy doesn't exist is that Leontes happens to be wrong. In the illusion of the play that jealousy is palpable to Leontes and no more or less existential than Othello's.

5. Frank Kermode, ed., *The Tempest* (The Arden Shakespeare) (London: Methuen and Co., 1961; first published 1954), p. liv.

6. P. lxxxii. Interestingly, when Kermode discusses the ostentatious observance of unity of time in *The Tempest,* one of the factors generally seen as calling attention to the fact that the play is a play, he

explains the phenomenon entirely in terms of the requirements of the play's action (p. lxxvi).

7. P. lxxxvii. Though he is speaking of *The Tempest,* his remarks are generally applicable, for there is a "basic modern version" of all of these plays as Kermode says there is of *The Tempest.*

8. An interesting analogy to some of the following remarks is found in the introduction by Hermann Broch to Rachel Bespaloff, *On the Iliad,* Bollingen series IX (New York: Pantheon Books, 1949), particularly Broch's discussion of "the style of old age."

9. Thomas Mann, *The Holy Sinner,* trans. H. T. Lowe-Porter (New York: Alfred A. Knopf, 1951), p. 94.

10. P. 98. Significantly "The Bad Children" is the title of the chapter that recounts the initial incest, and thus the phrase calls attention to Clemens' narrative.

11. "But to [the Pope's] blood the identity of wife and mother was familiar long before he learned the truth and play-acted about it" (p. 330). In the German text: "lange bevor er die Wahrheit erfuhr und sich gar komödiantisch darüber entsetzte" (*Der Erwählte,* Frankfurt: S. Fischer Verlag, 1951, p. 314).

12. P. 332. In the German, p. 316:

> "Und hat, lose Frau, nur Euer Spiel mit Uns getrieben?"
>
> "Da Ihr Euer Spiel mit mir treiben wolltet—"
>
> "Wir gedachten, Gott eine Unterhaltung damit zu bieten."
>
> "Dabei ging ich Euch gern zur Hand. Und doch war es kein Spiel."

13. *The Winter's Tale,* I.ii.186–188; III.ii.34–36, 27–28; V.ii.76–77; V.iii.151–155.

14. *Confessions of Felix Krull, Confidence Man,* trans. Denver Lindley (New York: Alfred A. Knopf, 1955), p. 253.

15. Pp. 20–21; cf. the episode of the circus and Felix's comments on it, pp. 189–195.

16. As I have argued elsewhere (*Shakespeare and the Common Understanding,* New York: The Free Press, 1967, pp. 192–237), Shakespeare's caprices on the relations between art and life only carry

to its conclusion in his last phase a concern that is evident even in early works like *The Taming of the Shrew* and *A Midsummer Night's Dream*. Similarly, in *The Holy Sinner* and *Confessions of Felix Krull* Mann recapitulates and develops anew a theme that, as is widely recognized, fascinated him throughout his entire career. In connection with the particular strategies of the two novels discussed here, it might be worth calling attention to the repeated motif in the *Joseph* series of the story as only a story, yet a story ordained by God, so that Laban, for example, acts as he does because he is playing a role (*Joseph and His Brothers,* trans. H. T. Lowe-Porter, New York: Alfred A. Knopf, 1948, p. 235); Joseph stages the reunion with his family as an entertainment for God ("All that is Egyptian go out from me . . . I invited God and the world to this play, but now shall God alone be witness" [p. 1114]), and summarizes his life as "only a play and a pattern" (p. 1207); and the end of the story (p. 1207) is a kind of symbolic transformation of its events into a novel composed on one level by God, on another by Mann: "Thus he spoke to them, and they laughed and wept together and stretched out their hands as he stood among them and touched him, and he too caressed them with his hands. And so endeth the beautiful story and God-invention [*die schöne Geschichte und Gotteserfindung*] of JOSEPH AND HIS BROTHERS."

17. *The Winter's Tale,* III.ii.81.

NOTES TO

MILTON: REVALUATIONS OF ROMANCE

BY BARBARA K. LEWALSKI

1. Among such works Milton's most frequent and most significant references are to: *The Faerie Queene;* Ariosto's *Orlando Furioso* which, in Harington's translation, Milton owned and carefully annotated; Boiardo's *Orlando Innamorato;* Tasso's *Gerusalemme Liberata;* and Malory's *Morte d'Arthur* which had gone through seven editions by 1650. Milton also refers occasionally to other works:

Chaucer's *Squire's Tale* in "Il Penseroso," ll. 109–115; Sidney's *Arcadia,* Francesco Moraes' *Palmerin of England* (1500–1572), *Amadis de Gaule* (14th century), Honore D'Urfe's *Astrée* (1610–1619), and Jorge Montemayor's *Diana* (1599) in *Eikonoklastes, Complete Prose Works of John Milton,* Vol. III, ed. Merritt Y. Hughes (New Haven, 1962), pp. 366–367; and Luigi Pulci's *Il Morgante Maggiore* (1481) in *Areopagitica, Prose Works,* Vol. II, ed. Ernest Sirluck (New Haven, 1959), p. 511. All references to Milton's prose, except to the *History of Britain,* are to this Yale University Press edition, general editor Don M. Wolfe.

2. E.g., Antonio Minturno, *L'Arte Poetica* (Venice, 1563), pp. 25–35; Filippo Sassetti, *Discorso Contro l'Ariosto,* cited in Bernard Weinberg, *A History of Literary Criticism,* 2 vols. (Chicago: University of Chicago Press, 1961), II, 971–976.

3. E.g., Giovambattista Geraldi Cinthio, *Discorso intorno al comporre dei romanzi* (Venice, 1554); Giovan Battista Pigna, *I romanzi* (Venice, 1554). See also Weinberg, *Literary Criticism,* I, 433–452.

4. *Prose Works,* Vol. I, ed. Don M. Wolfe (New Haven, 1953), p. 813.

5. Roger Ascham, *The Scholemaster* (1570), in G. Gregory Smith, ed., *Elizabethan Critical Essays,* 2 vols. (Oxford: Clarendon Press, 1904) I, 2–4:

These be the inchantementes of *Circes,* brought out of *Italie,* to marre mens maners in England; . . . In our forefathers tyme, whan Papistrie, as a standyng poole, covered and overflowed all England, fewe bookes were read in our tong, savying certaine bookes of Chevalrie . . . as one for example, *Morte Arthure;* the whole pleasure of which booke standeth in two speciall poyntes, in open mans slaughter and bold bawdrye: In which booke those be counted the noblest Knightes that do kill most men without any quarell, and commit fowlest aduoulteres by sutlest shiftes. . . . Yet I know when Gods Bible was banished the Court, and *Morte Arthure* received into the Princes chamber. . . . And yet ten *Morte Arthures* do not the tenth part so much harme as one of these bookes made in Italie and translated in England.

Henry Vaughan, "Preface," *Silex Scintillans* (1655), in L. C. Martin, ed., *Workes*, 2nd ed. (Oxford: Clarendon Press, 1957), p. 389:

> The most lascivious compositions of *France* and *Italy* are here *naturalized* and made *English:* And this . . . with so much favor and success, that nothing *takes* (as they rightly phrase it) like a *Romance.* . . . If *every idle word shall be accounted for,* and if *no corrupt communication should proceed out of our mouths,* how desperate (I beseech you) is their condition, who all their life time, and out of meer design, study *lascivious fictions.*

6. *Prose Works,* III, 364.

7. *Prose Works,* III, 362.

8. Frye, *Anatomy of Criticism* (New York: Atheneum, 1966), p. 153.

9. *Prose Works,* I, 890–891.

10. E.g., Lorenzo Gambara, *Tractatio de perfectae poëseos ratione* (Rome, 1576); Andrew Segni, *Ragionamento . . . Sopra le cose pertinenti, alla Poetica* (Florence, 1581). See also Weinberg, *Literary Criticism,* I, 299–310. Sir John Harington, in the "Apologie of Poetrie" which prefaces his translation of *Orlando Furioso,* felt obliged to defend poetry in general and the *Orlando* in particular from sweeping Platonic charges denouncing it as "a nurse of lies, a pleaser of fooles, a breeder of dangerous errors, and an inticer to wantonnesse."

11. *Paradise Lost* I.579–580. All citations of Milton's poetry are from *Complete Poetry and Major Prose,* ed. Merritt Y. Hughes (New York, Odyssey, 1957). *Of Reformation, Prose Works,* I, 560; *Eikonoklastes, Prose Works,* III, 390.

12. *Areopagitica, Prose Works,* II, 516.

13. *Commonplace Book, Prose Works,* I, 385–386, 418, 391–392.

14. *Anatomy of Criticism,* pp. 186–187.

15. *Odyssey,* Book X; *Orlando Furioso,* cantos VI–VII; *Gerusalemme Liberata,* Books XIV–XVI; *Faerie Queene* II.xii.

16. *Faerie Queene* III.xii.

17. *Ibid.* I.i–iii.

18. *Ibid.* II.x.14–19; cf. Ariosto, *Orlando,* canto VII.

19. *Faerie Queene* I.vi.1–19.

20. Erich Auerbach, *Mimesis: The Representation of Reality in Western Literature,* trans. Willard Trask (Garden City, N.Y.: Doubleday, 1957), pp. 116–119, defines the conventional romance ethos as follows:

> [The knight] sets out without mission or office; he seeks adventure, that is, perilous encounters by which he can prove his mettle. . . . The fearless hero . . . by strength, virtue, cunning, and the help of God, overcomes . . . dangers and frees others from them. . . . Trial through adventure is the real meaning of the knight's ideal existence. . . . The world of knightly proving is a world of adventure. . . . It is a world specifically created and designed to give a knight opportunity to prove himself.

21. Cf. Rev. xiii, describing the great Beast warring with and persecuting the followers of the Lamb, and their endurance in hope: "Here is the patience and the faith of the Saints" (verse 10).

22. The Happy Gardens of Milton's Epilogue allude to Spenser's Garden of Adonis, and that allusion reinforces the difference between the two poets' visions. Spenser's Venus and Adonis in company with Cupid and Psyche and all other lovers epitomize the natural perfection and fruition of the garden of generation:

> There wont faire *Venus* often to enjoy
> Her deare *Adonis* joyous company,
> And reape sweet pleasure of the wanton boy; . . .
> There now he liveth in eternall blis,
> Joying his goddesse, and of her enjoyd: . . .
> For that wilde Bore, the which him once anoyd,
> She firmely hath emprisoned for ay. (III.vi.46–48)

Milton's image, by contrast, is of Nature partially restored, mending but not yet mended:

> Beds of Hyacinth and Roses
> Where young Adonis oft reposes,
> Waxing well of his deep wound
> In slumber soft, and on the ground
> Sadly sits th' *Assyrian* Queen. (998–1002)

Only in the realm "far above" is nature perfectly restored and fruition

attained: there the Celestial Cupid hold his dear Psyche "sweet en-
tranc't" and the blissful twins Youth and Joy are born.

23. *Prose Works,* I, 495; "Mansus" ll. 80–83. Cf. "Epitaphium
Damonis," ll. 162–168.

24. Such sources as Geoffrey of Monmouth, Nennius, Gildas,
William of Malmesbury, and James Buchanan. I accept W. R.
Parker's argument as to the time of composition of the first four
chapters; see *Milton: A Biography,* 2 vols. (Oxford: Clarendon Press,
1968), I, 326–338; II, 939 (n. 69).

25. *The History of Britain,* in *The Works of John Milton,* ed.
F. A. Patterson, et al., 18 vols. (New York: Columbia University Press,
1932), X, 128.

26. Cf. *Paradise Lost* III.422–497; *Orlando Furioso,* canto XXXIV,
stanzas 71–85.

27. A. Bartlett Giamatti points to Romance sources of Milton's
Eden but draws different conclusions as to the effects these echoes
produce in Milton's poem, *The Earthly Paradise and the Renaissance
Epic* (Princeton: Princeton University Press, 1966), pp. 295–355. See
also John M. Steadman, *Milton and the Renaissance Hero* (Oxford:
Clarendon Press, 1967), pp. 108–136.

28. The special character of Milton's Garden is argued more fully
in my "Innocence and Experience in Milton's Eden," in Thomas
Kranidas, ed., *New Essays on "Paradise Lost"* (Berkeley: University
of California Press, 1969), pp. 86–117. See also J. M. Evans, *"Paradise
Lost" and the Genesis Tradition* (Oxford: Clarendon Press, 1968),
pp. 242–271.

29. *Paradise Lost* IV.624–632:

> With first approach of light, we must be ris'n,
> And at our pleasant labor, to reform
> Yon flow'ry Arbors, yonder Alleys green,
> Our walk at noon, with branches overgrown,
> That mock our scant manuring, and require
> More hands than ours to lop thir wanton growth:
> Those Blossoms also, and those dropping Gums,

That lie bestrown unsightly and unsmooth,
Ask riddance, if we mean to tread with ease.

30. In this Adam contrasts with those foolish knights in Ariosto's *Orlando Furioso,* canto XLIII, who design a trial by absence to test their wives' fidelity.

31. *Paradise Regained* III.338–339. Cf. Boiardo, *Orlando Innamorato* I.x.26.

32. *Paradise Regained* IV.541–542. Cf. *Orlando Furioso,* trans. Harington, canto IV, stanzas 13, 35–38.

33. Trans. Edward Fairfax (1600), ed. J. C. Nelson (New York, 1963), Book X, stanza 64.

34. Thomas Malory, *Morte d'Arthur,* Book XI, chapter ii; Book VIII; Book XVII, chapters xiii–xvi, ed. John Rhys, 2 vols. (London: J. M. Dent; New York: E. P. Dutton, 1967), II, 126–135, 254–260.

35. *Morte d'Arthur* (Book IV, chapters xxi–xxiii), I, 118–123.

36. *Ibid.* (Book XIV, chapters viii–x), II, 201–205.

37. The genre question is discussed at length in my *Milton's Brief Epic* (Providence, R.I.: Brown University Press, and London: Methuen, 1966).